DISABLED 101

Adult Onset Disability in an Ableist World

MJ Kuhn
L Kuhn

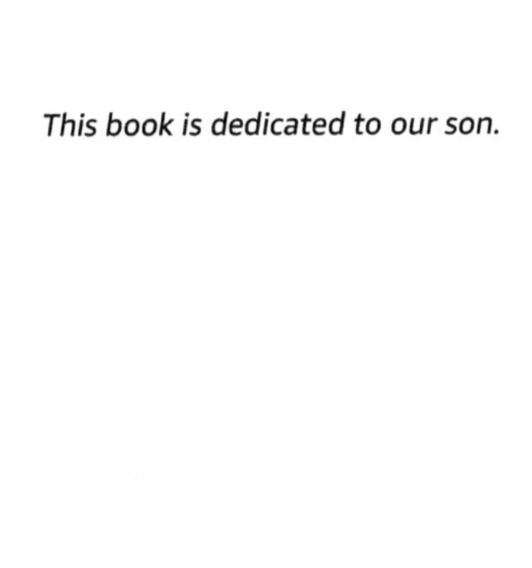

This book is dedicated to our son.

CONTENTS

Privacy and Professional Services Disclaimers

All the names and identifying details of the people and organizations in this book have been changed to protect their privacy and to ensure they are completely unidentifiable. However, every example in this book has an underlying principle that has been directly experienced multiple times.

The concepts in this book are intended as a self-help support based on the writers' views and are not intended to replace psychological treatment, medical treatment, or employment services. The reader should see a medical professional should they have concerns regarding their well-being or medical condition, or an employment specialist regarding their vocational pursuits.

PROLOGUE

WTF Happened?

No one plans for an Adult Onset Disability. Not really. You may know about genetic risks and family histories. You may quickly recite this information to your family doctor, who has limited control over whether these conditions will one day show themselves. Or perhaps you are in an accident or some other event occurs. Nonetheless, the lottery of life decides, and one day you may wake up with a relatively serious impairment that leads to a disability. Or maybe you already have.

Well, I have. Or did. And I am living with a medical condition resulting in impairments, and disabilities. In my forties, I was diagnosed with advanced stage 4 melanoma. I almost died due to the severity of the medical condition, and I almost died twice due to side effects of the immunotherapy treatment. I have ongoing symptoms due to the immunotherapy that have resulted in disabilities.

My cancer is stable, for now, and I'm relatively healthy. Disabled and healthy? How can you be disabled and healthy? These are contradictory terms for much of the general public. We'll get into that. We'll also get into disabled and content! Shocker right? Few of the typical people would believe it.

Now You

You may have been in a car or workplace accident and now have a physical impairment. Maybe you caught Covid-19 and now face the symptomatology of long Covid with no real treatment available. You may have had the onset of bipolar disorder, with symptoms of mania and depression. You may have had a physical impairment and noticed some change in how your body was working and went through the scary, long process of seeing specialist after specialist to even get a diagnosis. Perhaps you developed arthritis, fibromyalgia, visual or hearing impairment, had a brain injury, or a stroke. There is a long list of medical impairments that can occur to us as adults that can cause disabilities. Whatever happened you are now faced with a new life with a disability.

Any change in our body or mind's functioning that results in a limitation can be hard to accept. In the end, it is you who will face it. You may need to adjust and learn to adapt, learn to accept, learn to accept help, learn new roles and new identities…and you never asked for any of it.

I get it. I've been through it.

For many of us, a disability causes distress. Some people adapt well without too much effort and have healthy accepting attitudes about their new level of abilities.

Then there is the rest of us. The ones who need to work at having a good attitude, to work at developing a healthy new disabled self-identity. The ones who need to intentionally work on redefining themselves as people with Adult Onset Disabilities who have a positive view of themselves and their futures.

This book has been designed to support people with Adult Onset Disabilities in changing and empowering their lives. It can be helpful if we plan for our future selves and think about the changes we would like to make. To move forward with an end in mind. It also recognizes that people with disabilities are all unique. This is a book where you take what works for you and leave the rest. Like a cafeteria.

The concepts in this book are intended to serve as a guide on how to adapt, accept, and thrive with an Adult Onset Disability. It should be noted that this guide will support people to the degree that they want and to the extent that they are able.

This guide has core principles called Guideposts in each

chapter. You may already know of some or all of the concepts. Now that your life is different, there are ways that you can view things differently, act differently, and get the things you want for your new life. The Guideposts serve to point out important concepts.

You Are Always Whole

Whether or not we want or need to work on ourselves post-disability, we are never not whole. Without doing anything. Right now. You and I are whole.

Everyone's story is different, but there are commonalities we are all faced with. The first commonality for a book intended for people with Adult Onset Disability is that you, the reader, developed a medical condition as an adult that resulted in a disability.

And that's where we will start...

PART I - KNOWLEDGE

There is no wealth like knowledge and no
poverty like ignorance – Buddha

1. THE NEW LIFE

As an adult, when we are hit with whatever mechanism that caused a medical impairment it is a shock. Whether or not you see it coming. If you lose functioning in part of your mind or body, you notice, and it is traumatic. We go through the grief process of moving in and out of the stages of shock/anger, depression, bargaining, and eventual acceptance. Coming to terms with your medical condition, its impairments, and adapting to your new functioning is a huge and important topic. How difficult and long this process is for an individual, varies greatly. Just like no two people are the same, no two people have the same experience.

Adapting to the psychological shock of an Adult Onset Disability, however, is not the focus of this book. Working through the factors at play after the onset of an Adult Onset Disability can be a very fragile process. If this is where you are at, make sure you are connected and have support. Contact your physician, hospital social workers, or distress phone lines in your community to get connected to resources to help you. For many people, a therapist who specializes in counselling for Adult Onset Disability is a good option.

This book assumes that you've had some time to psychologically adjust to your new self with your medical condition and impairment. It assumes that your condition is stable or, if it is a progressive condition, that you have had some short-term stability or 'breathing' room to process how you want to live the rest of your new life. Now it's time to start looking at what you are faced with and what you want out of the rest of your life.

I'd like to highlight this next part: There are fantastic people out there. There are incredible people in the medical system, remarkable people in government services, supportive peers, and wonderful people in the community who view people with disabilities in very respectful and helpful ways. There are some outstanding, kind people in almost all organizations and walks of life. I have been blessed with having some of them in my immediate family and in my circle of friends. I am stating this now as throughout the book I am not going to sugarcoat the prevalence of Ableism in our world. Much like how incredibly patronizing and hurtful it would be to minimize racism; it would be as hurtful and patronizing to minimize the Ableism that happens. I'm going to be real about Ableism, and I pull no punches. Let's just make a point now of not forgetting that we can always find some good people out there. It is just a fact that presently much of society views people with disabilities in ignorant and unhelpful ways. We'll get into that. We're going to really get into the macro and micro presence of Ableism, but for now, let's look at a definition to get on the same page.

Accessliving.org in their Ableism 101 online article, defines Ableism as:

> Ableism is the discrimination of and social prejudice against people with disabilities based on the belief that typical abilities are superior. At its heart, ableism is rooted in the assumption that disabled people require 'fixing' and defines people by their disability. (Eisenmenger, 2022)

Ableism sucks. It just does. However, there is a lot of helpful knowledge and great strategies to help deal with Ableism. More about that later on.

Back to me

In a way, it's ironic. I've worked with people with a wide variety of physical, mental, and cognitive disabilities over 20 years. After having been on the professional side of the desk for a career and then having to go through the medical, government and insurance systems for cancer treatment has been bizarre. More than bizarre, actually. It's been surreal, deva-vuish, and a bit metaphysical.

In my 20s I completed a degree in Disability Studies and over the next two decades worked in many roles in disability services. I worked at vocational training centres, day programs and group homes for people with developmental disabilities and/or mental health conditions. My wife and I worked as supportive (paid) roommates for people with various disabilities who lived with us. I worked at a College as an Educational and Career advisor for students with disabilities, and as a case manager for short-term disability insurance benefits. Finally, the last four years of my working life, I worked as an insurance medical adjudicator determining medical eligibility for disability benefits.

I've done a pretty wide scope of jobs. I've seen quite a lot within services for people with disabilities. I've seen some uplifting stuff in these jobs. People with disabilities and their workers doing some pretty cool stuff for each other and their communities. I've also seen some really sickening stuff of making very disabled people jumping some ridiculous hoops. Sometimes this hoop-jumping happens because of necessary bureaucracy, sometimes because of professional laziness or incompetence, and sometimes out of politics. Oppression of people with disabilities of varying intensities and contexts is very real, and it usually exists in some form (often unintentionally) in organizations. Wherever there are groups of people, organizations, and systems, there is Ableism. The sad fact is that Ableism is embedded in North American culture, which permeates into our organizations.

When I developed cancer, I had to go through some of the very same hoops that I had helped my clients navigate. The experience of going through the systems as a disabled person is very different from going through it as the helping professional. I had a few good experiences navigating systems as the 'client'. However, developing a disability resulted in a lot of difficult identity-based experiences for me. Things that gave me pause for thought, things that made me sick to my stomach, and things that weren't ethically right. Having the background I did, made it easier for me. For sure. I understood the systems, the available financial supports, medical systems in my communities. I usually knew which service or support was worth pursuing and which was not, based on my professional knowledge.

Nonetheless, for me personally, developing an Adult Onset Disability was like being smacked in the face with a door. The impairment was challenging, but it was the social impacts of Ableism that was often the door. The identity shifting changes I had to go through smacked me. As well as the eventual disappearance of some friends and family members.

Now that things have settled, and I have Intentionally Shifted my beliefs, identities, and activities towards a new way of life; I can say my post disability-onset life has resulted in many good things. I was able to pursue my lifelong passion of music, pursue an interest in history, renewed a clearer sense of spirituality, connected with my family in new and meaningful ways. It also gave me flexibility to develop this book from my journals. However, these good things occurred after the Ableism door smacked me down countless times.

Back then the Ableism door reaffirmed to me the fact that I needed to find a new way of thinking, believing, and living.

2. A CONTENT LIFE
WITH DIGNITY

I am not an expert. In fact, I am wary of anyone who considers themselves an expert. As mentioned in the previous chapter, I have employment experience in disability services and related education. More importantly, I have navigated many systems as a person with disabilities. Ultimately, this is where I feel I've gotten the most expertise. Some of my conclusions will not be a great surprise. You won't always hear yourself gasping with amazement at all the points as you read this book. Some of it is downright obvious. However, these points are important enough that they need to be made.

Through my combined professional and personal experiences with disabilities, I've learned indispensable things that have been highlighted as Guideposts. Guideposts are intended to serve as core concepts to aid the reader's understanding of the ideas. Guideposts are also intended to act as a reference tool to assist the reader in intentionally redefining or shifting themselves for the future they want as a person with an Adult Onset Disability. The first Guidepost is a description of a 'way of being'. It is a belief, a way of carrying oneself, and an ongoing goal that many people with Adult Onset Disabilities may benefit from. This guidepost can be helpful for the reader to centre on as a first step.

Guidepost 1

To Live a Dignified, Content Life as a Person
with an Adult Onset Disability

No one is happy all the time about everything. Happiness is elusive, and expectations for being happy seem to constantly change. Being content, on the other hand, means being ok with your life, identities, and roles. It means you go through the ups and downs we all have and have a healthy self-concept, some resiliency, and generally enjoy your life. Dignity is important. Due to Ableism and the self-stigmatization that often results, adopting dignity as a core value is critical.

Merriam-Webster's online dictionary lists dignity as the quality or state of being worthy, honoured, or esteemed. Historically, people with disabilities have not been treated in this manner. That being said, I think it is safe to say that most people in general would want to live a content life with dignity.

The value of personal dignity within the first Guidepost is the one that I used for my own Intentional Shifting. I suggest that you adopt this Guidepost or modify it to suit you. I encourage you to add whatever values to it that make this 'way of being statement' powerful for you. For example, you can add spiritual elements, add commitments to your spouse or family, your legacy or any other elements that are truly meaningful for you. However, within the statement I recommend keeping the concepts of dignity, you, and the Adult Onset Disability. Like a personal mission statement, the first Guidepost is ground zero at the beginning of your Intentional Shift process.

3. DISABLED 101

Disabled 101. Catchy hey? Like a college class, though very different. Disabled 101 is the passing on of Guidepost concepts intended to enhance and empower the lives of people with Adult Onset Disabilities.

Take What Works for You and Leave the Rest

People with disabilities are just that; people. There is an infinite combination of experiences, cultures, types of disabilities, intersections, values, beliefs, etc in the disabled group. There are so many differences in this group of people that no one book or set of concepts could possibly apply to everyone. That being said, many people who have Adult Onset Disabilities have commonalities in their life experience. The concepts in this book are intended to try to help disabled people enhance their lives while keeping these commonalities in mind. The Guideposts are intended to serve as key elements and reminders. However, nothing here is written in stone. All concepts can be individualized and tailored for the person. If one Guidepost or concept doesn't speak to you, ignore it or develop one that is similar that works for you.

Disabled 101 is primarily a tool to help disabled people move themselves into a more empowered life, while valuing and respecting others. Again, take what works for you and leave the rest.

Let's start with the word 'disabled'. Terminology used to describe our population has come a long way. Presently, respectful terms such as disabled people or people with disabilities are often used.

Labelling words for marginalized groups have different narratives and historical beliefs behind them. One of the worst old words for our population is 'cripple'. It is just a nasty word. The word cripple evokes sad images from the early 1900s of people having difficulty walking (if they could walk at all), in abject poverty, begging, unable to communicate, and carrying an aura of contagion. In the past, the word cripple was often used to describe people with physical disabilities. Medical personnel in the past used this word freely with patients to describe their disabilities or to classify people. 'Your legs are crippled' or 'Your child will always be a cripple' are two offensive examples. Civil rights movements and language sensitivity have slowly pulled these nasty words out of our vocabulary. Other offensive nasty words that I'm glad have left our vocabulary include: gimp, invalid, spastic, retard, and lame.

Often in language, there is a value and meaning behind the words we choose. The values in the preceding offensive terms consist of being 'inferior, damaged or less worthy'. Over time and through social activism, the values have shifted to focus on the worth of the person: person with a disability or disabled person. These changes in terminology reflect how far the disability movement has come, though there is still a long way to go.

It should be noted that some disability activists have reclaimed offensive words such as cripple or crip. The Critical Disability Studies Collective from the University of Minnesota writes in their online terminology section,

> Crip: A term used historically to stigmatize and oppress disabled people. It has been reclaimed by some disabled people. It should only be used with permission from the community or person who is being referred to.

How many of us are there?

As per the United Nations, people with disabilities comprise the largest minority group in the world. Around 10 percent of the world's population, or 650 million people, live with a disability. This includes congenital (born with) and Adult Onset Disabilities. The World Health Organization (2022) puts this number at 15% or 1 billion people!

As you can see, there are a lot of us, and we are not going away. In fact, our numbers are growing as our population ages and the baby boomers become seniors with disabilities. Disabilities affect most of us at some stage of our lives, either temporarily or permanently. At any one time, 1 in 5 people in North America have a mental health diagnosis. As we grow into our older years, medical conditions and disabilities become much more prevalent. It is very common to see older people using canes, wheelchairs, and scooters which indicate mobility disabilities.

There are also many definitions for disability that are influenced by values and contexts. How a person defines disability has big implications for their life. In a later chapter, I'll get into Disability Lens or Models.

A good definition of disability is from The United Nations' Convention on the Rights of Persons with Disabilities (CRPD, 2008) that states:

> Disability is an evolving concept, and that disability results from the interaction between persons with impairments and attitudinal and environmental barriers that hinder their full and effective participation in society on an equal basis with others.

It is a common misperception that people with disabilities are a static group with unchanging membership. Many people falsely believe that most disabled people are born with their conditions. There is also the belief that most 'typical people' will never become disabled and that all disabilities can be seen. The truth is, developing an Adult Onset Disability is very common. Examples include the onset of a medical condition leading to a disability through long Covid, car/bike accidents, workplace accidents, heart diseases/stroke, and conditions associated with aging. Adult Onset Disabilities can be temporary (like breaking a leg) or permanent (like developing progressive multiple sclerosis). Invisible disabilities are common and will be addressed in a later chapter.

Disability affects almost everyone in their lifetimes to some degree. It directly impacts people when they develop a disability themselves. It indirectly impacts people when one of their loved ones or friends develops a disability.

Disability Movement in Brief

In North America, the status of disabled people has come a long way, but not by accident and not easily. Like any social change, it has been fought for by disabled people, their families, and their supporters over many decades. The ADL (2015), a leading anti-hate organization, reports that disability advocacy groups have used many strategies for change. These strategies include lobbying governments, increasing social awareness, protests, civil disobedience, advocacy groups, media attention, and having a united front with other minority movements (such as Black Lives Matter and LGBTQ+ groups).

The development of academic departments (including Disability Studies), and the development of advanced theories of disability (Disability Justice) have greatly helped in the legitimacy of the movement and provided frameworks for understanding disability issues.

The disability movement has resulted in positive civil rights changes. These changes are reflected in the recognition of people with disabilities in legislation throughout the developed world. These changes in legislation are monumental milestones, but are not endpoints. They serve as legal mechanisms through which people with disabilities can legally challenge discriminations. The work of Disability Justice in part is the evolution of the disability movement (centred on queer, black, brown and indigenous persons' perspectives) and evolved partly from the inadequacies of the civil rights movements. More will be covered on Disability Justice later in the book.

There are already many excellent books out there about the history of civil rights movement of people with disabilities. I encourage readers to learn the key events. Civil rights movements serve as mechanisms for legal and social change. The recent development of Disability Justice is a great shift towards progress in the fight for equality and respect for people with disabilities.

But we are not nearly there yet.

4. MY CANCER AND DISABILITY ONSET STORY

Having worked in disability services for many years, I thought I had seen all sides of North America's present treatment of people with disabilities. However, I learned, you can never truly understand something until you experience it firsthand. Which I did.

My Cancer Story

The summer of 2018 my family and I were very active. We went camping frequently and usually went for a hike every 2nd weekend. I was going to the gym three times a week and being in my forties was trying to reach a goal of attaining my highest level of physical fitness. I started having trouble breathing during the hikes and at the gym. A visit to the walk-in medical clinic resulted in asthma puffers that did nothing to help. On my third trip to the walk-in clinic, I was sent for a chest x-ray. A week later, I received the results from the stunned doctor. Two masses were identified in my lungs. One mass was the size of a large orange and the other the size of a cherry. After a few agonizing weeks and multiple tests, I was diagnosed with stage 4 metastatic melanoma.

After the stage 4 diagnosis, I was referred to the local cancer centre and waited for my appointment. During this time I lost significant weight, strength, energy, and hope. A month later, I completed a PET scan that found the chest tumour had reached a size of 9 cm x 9 cm by 5 cm, about the size of a small cantaloupe. The smaller one had grown to 4 cm x 4 cm x 3 cm. By cancer centre standards, these tumours were massive. However, that wasn't all. The PET scan found multiple tumours in my lungs, leg muscle, spleen, rib, leg bones, and other areas. The melanoma cancer was metastasizing out of control. When I saw the oncologist, she didn't convey much hope.

I can write about it factually now. Then, of course, I was a mess. The event devastated every aspect of my life. Luckily, I have a wonderful wife, great family and a few good friends who stood by me throughout the worst of the illness.

After seeing the oncologist, I immediately started nivolumab and ipilimumab therapy, which were two newer immunotherapy intravenous medications at the time. What immunotherapy does is twofold. It helps the immune system to recognize cancer and accelerates it to attack the cancer. Unfortunately, the immune system gets so ramped up, it attacks the healthy parts of the body as well. I ended up in hospital on many occasions, and dealt with significant medical impairments and disabilities.

I reacted extremely well to the immunotherapy, and over the next year many of the cancer sites disappeared entirely or shrunk to small sizes. The cancer reached a point of stability where I was able to return to work part-time. It was however a temporary success. Six months later the cancer started regrowing, and I had to leave work and start immunotherapy again.

Ironically and lucky for me, having severe side effects to immunotherapy is associated with good outcomes. And I have had an excellent outcome. At the time of writing, I have been told that I have what is referred to as a complete response. This means that the immunotherapy worked and there is no evidence of cancer in my body. The hope is that the cancer is cured. If the cancer growth starts again, it will be treated like a chronic condition with more immunotherapy. This will go on for the rest of my life. Surviving three very close brushes with death has given me plenty to reflect on. The toxicity of the immunotherapy damaged my pituitary gland causing hypophysitis which means the pituitary doesn't initiate production of cortisol anymore. I take medication to replace the cortisol. However, I still experience fatigue as the cortisol is not nearly as effective as a normally functioning pituitary gland.

My primary medical conditions are now stage 4 melanoma-complete response, colitis, and hypophysitis. Symptoms from these medical conditions that result in disability include poor stamina, easily fatigued, short-term memory problems, occasional confusion, daily nausea, and headaches. Last, but not least, I have unpredictable immunotherapy flare-ups (called immune related adverse events: irAE). irAE is when my immune system ramps up for no reason and starts attacking different body systems. This leaves me exhausted for days at a time, with muscle aches and pains, inability to concentrate, and nausea. These flare-ups happen every few weeks and last several days. These episodic events typically knock me out of commission.

When you see me on a good day, you would not know I have a disability. My disabilities are invisible. That being said, having gone through advanced stage 4 metastatic cancer, hypophysitis, colitis, and the severe ongoing immune related adverse events, I very much have multiple disabilities.

I went through the worst of stage 4 cancer and I survived. My medical conditions and disabilities are ongoing, but I am on the other side. That being said, cancer is cancer and could return at any time with a vengeance.

With that in mind, I have had to do a lot of thinking and accepting about my life and my future. I have come to terms with my present health and unknown future. I have accepted being limited by the symptoms of the side effects of treatment, to the extent I could not work. I accepted the limitations in energy. I accepted the losses of roles and identities. This was the beginning stages of my personal transformation or Intentional Shifting of my beliefs. It involved a lot of acceptance and facing forward.

However, there are some things I could not accept. I could not accept being crippled by the attitudes and opinions of others.

I could not accept the discrimination/Ableism that would deny my ability to develop myself. I could not accept the Ableism that caused isolation and lack of community. I could not accept the Ableism interfering with my self-concept and interfering with the way I wanted to live as a dignified and content person with an Adult Onset Disability.

This is a common challenge for many people with Adult Onset Disabilities. We venture out in the world to live our lives and accommodate our disabilities. To accomplish this we have to reorganize our whole lives: our jobs and finances (or lack thereof), our ongoing relationship with the medical system, our friends/ family, our newfound abilities, our discovery of strengths we didn't know we had. However, as people with new Adult Onset Disabilities, we face a new obstacle that we likely never faced when we were typical or able-bodied people. The obstacle of Ableism.

In my view, almost any conversation of disability has an Ableism context that should be addressed. There is a false view in North American culture that the lives of people with disabilities are tragic and should be viewed as deficient and inferior compared to typical people. This embedded Ableist view is so overwhelmingly present in day-to-day life, that the belief is viewed as obvious, correct, and as a cultural norm. This view, also known as the Tragedy/Deficiency/Charity Model, is discussed in detail in an upcoming chapter. It is worth noting that some people are not Ableist at all. These are the people who respect and value people with disabilities as regular people. It is also worth noting, that most people who are Ableist are not intentionally so, but hold false beliefs due to lack of knowledge, indifference, or not being exposed to more progressive beliefs about disability. There is a lot to Ableism, and it is discussed more fully in a later chapter. Most people understand what racism or sexism is. People from minority groups or women (or both) may, unfortunately, be familiar with discrimination. Ableism is as damaging as racism and sexism or any of the other 'isms'. However, Ableism is poorly understood in the world and even by some disability communities.

We as people with Adult Onset Disabilities have to understand Ableism. We need to recognize the impact Ableism can have on our lives. This knowledge allows us to Intentionally Shift our awareness. With this in mind, we can gently strategize for Ableism so that we can accomplish our goals and live the lives we want and deserve.

Most importantly, we don't have to view the world or ourselves through the derogatory lens of Ableism. Lenses, or models, are how we all view the world. Once you understand disability lenses and learn you can pick your lens, things can really start to open up. We'll get into that in more detail later.

5. THE VALUE IN THE DIVERSITY OF HUMANITY

This chapter title might sound very esoteric to you. The Value in the Diversity of Humanity at first glance sounds like some hoity-toity term from some academic writer in an ivory tower. Some vague philosophical concept. This statement, in fact, is a very practical and important concept. I didn't invent this phrase. The concept of valuing diversity has been around for many decades. The racial minority and feminist movements have been instrumental in promoting this concept. Additionally, folx from the LGBTQ+ and black civil rights movements have been embracing the inclusivity of diversity since the 1970s and before. However, recognizing disability in the diversity spectrum is relatively new. (MIUSA, 2022)

Disability is as essential to human diversity as any of the other groups. There is value in all of humanity, be they marginalized or non-marginalized groups, majority, or minority.

The statement 'The Value in the Diversity of Humanity' may seem just like a few written words. However, these few words can be powerful and can be the backdrop for the core values of a person's life. Believing and living this Guidepost as a basic principle of life, allows people with disabilities to have equal footing with everyone else.

The second guidepost of this book is to 'Recognize the Value in the Diversity of Humanity'. To break this down, this phrase means that there is a wide range of people that make up humanity. There are young, middle age and older people. There are people of varying ethnicities. People of varying sexual orientations, gender and gender expressions, and combinations thereof. People of different heights, weights, and muscle/fat composition. There are low, middle, and high-income people. There are people with different levels of education. People who work 70+ hours a week, people who work full-time, people who work part-time and people who do not work at all. There are people who have medical impairments who do not have disabilities and of course, there are people who have disabilities.

The belief in this Guidepost is that we as human beings value them all. Period. We don't have to like everyone, but everyone in every group has inherent human value. Everyone has one unit of worth. It has to be highlighted that just as all people within the diversity of races have value, so do people within the diversity of disabilities.

Everyone has value. Including me and Including You.

Why is this so important? This is an essential belief because it is a foundation belief that promotes the dignity and worth of people with disabilities alongside the rest of humanity. It's the block on the bottom of the Jenga game stack. The foundation that everything is built on. Without this foundation, everything else falls down.

When we only value certain groups of people, we end up treating people very differently. How we value other groups of people determines many things.

For example, whether or not you believe in 'Recognize the Value in the Diversity of Humanity' will determine:

- Who gets served in a restaurant
- If some groups have to be segregated in schools, public transportation, housing, swimming pools, or at drinking fountains
- Who can run for office and get elected
- Who can apply for and be hired for a job
- Who you will be friends with

- Who you will 'allow' your teenage son or daughter to date
- Who you will let cut in front of you in traffic
- Who will use which bathroom
- Which organization you will donate money to
- How government policy should prioritize social spending
- What should be taught in schools about which groups of people

As you can see, beliefs about people impact attitudes and behaviours towards groups. I would guess that most people have some variation of the 'Recognize the Value in the Diversity of Humanity' belief, but with some group exclusions. A racist example of a variation of this belief is: Value everyone, except Chinese people.

The variation I'm proposing of 'Recognize the Value in the Diversity of Humanity' is inclusive of everyone.

What about drug dealers, and people who break laws? What about people engaging in activities that we may not support, like vaping or smoking tobacco?

The response is that despite inclusive valuing, we still need laws to protect us. We also require street smarts to ensure our safety. We still require no smoking signs on planes and in hotel rooms. There needs to be legal consequences and rehabilitation for drug dealers and other people who have broken laws. However, the inclusive philosophy of 'Recognize the Value in the Diversity of Humanity' sees these people as human beings who each have one unit of value. These people who each have one unit of value may need humanistic rehabilitation, but they still have value. Again, there is no requirement that you like everyone or that you agree with everyone's actions. Just that all human beings have inherent equal value.

To a lesser degree, vapers and tobacco smokers may engage in unhealthy and socially unpopular activities. I may not agree with the activities, and I promote educating people on health risks and providing drug cessation programs; but that none of that relates to the human value that these folx have.

Adopting some type of belief of the value of all people serves as a platform for the rest of the Guideposts to be based on. Ultimately, this core belief serves as the basis for the reader's Intentional Shift activities. Don't worry too much about this now. It will fall into place as we go.

Guidepost 2

Recognize the Value in the Diversity of Humanity

6. DISABILITY MODELS AND WHY THEY ARE SO IMPORTANT

Hey, don't worry. I'm not dragging you down into a dull psychology or linguistics course. There are just a few terms and definitions that we have to be on the same page with. You may know them already, and if you don't, they are not complex. To understand this book and to truly understand disability, you have to understand what models are and the different disability model definitions. A model is just a theoretical lens that you pick to view the world. These models or lenses have different contexts and values.

The models described here are:

1. Medical Model of Disability

2. Tragedy/Deficiency/Charity Model of Disability

3. Social Model of Disability

4. Super-Disabled Model

The Medical Model

The Medical Model is a common model for looking at disability. It holds the view that health is the absence of illness. This model sees an individual with a medical condition as requiring medical intervention to 'cure' them back into a normal state. If a cure is not possible, then the goal becomes minimizing the impairment to lessen any disability.

The Medical Model views disability in terms of unfortunate medical outcomes, sickness, and lack of function. The model views the disabled person as broken, abnormal and needing medical repair to make them normal again. In this view, the individual and their medical condition is viewed as the source of the disability.

The Tragedy/Deficiency/Charity Model of Disability

The Tragedy, Deficiency, Charity Model is likely the most common model when viewing disability. It understands medical condition and disability as interchangeable terms. It views people with disabilities as objects of pity that are deficient and require charity. I'm not just referring to financial charity. I'm talking about attitudinal charity and emotional charity. In North America this belief stems in part from years gone by when the church cared for severely disabled people, orphaned children and elderly people. It was widely understood that without the charity of the church, the marginalized groups listed would suffer tragically and then cease to exist. Today, the Tragedy/Deficiency/Charity Model views people with disabilities as inferior when compared to 'superior' able-bodied people. This model focuses on disabled people's inabilities and deficits. This contrasts with focusing on disabled people's abilities and providing supports and accommodations that would enable them to thrive. The Deficiency/Tragedy/Charity model is insidious and deeply rooted in North American culture and beliefs. It is often hidden and built-in within cultural norms and policies. Some people with this view hold extreme beliefs, to the degree that they see the disabled as a subclass of humans to be tolerated and kept out of sight.

The Deficiency/Tragedy/Charity Model drives the belief that it is a necessary evil to provide the disabled with government funding and services. This support is viewed as necessary not to help the disabled community, but to minimize social disharmony. This model framework can be subtle and is frequently patronizing for the disabled. It is sometimes used unconsciously by well-meaning people who try to be 'nice' to a disabled person in a condescending and pitying manner.

Back to Me

When I was in the terminal stages of stage 4 melanoma, I had cancer tumours in most of my major body systems. I was extraordinarily ill and weak. I was fortunate as I received an outpouring of support from friends, family and coworkers in cards, emails, and phone calls. People were expressing condolences for my illness and my likely pending demise. A lot of this was genuine kindness and compassion. It helped me to know I was cared about, that people were thinking of me, and that people were praying for me. It was a wonderful display of humanity, for which I am still grateful. Unfortunately, I found that sometimes this goodwill was coupled with a 'thank God that's not happening to me' attitude. Worse of all, sometimes it was coupled with traces of pity.

I am sure you can see why people with disabilities would not want the Tragedy/Deficiency/Charity Model to be the framework through which they are viewed, treated or as the basis for government policy. Who would want their entire post-Adult Onset Disability life to be viewed as a tragedy?

Scenario

Let's look at an example to see how it can be helpful for one model to shift into another. I'll use the example of Bob, who became a double leg amputee due to an accident. Following the accident, Bob goes through a major change in functioning. He goes through multiple medical procedures and deals with struggle and physical pain. In the Tragedy/Deficiency/Charity model, this is where Bob's story would end. He is forevermore a tragic case requiring financial and attitudinal charity.

In reality, this Adult Onset Disability event is a continuation of Bob's life story. This person who is a double leg amputee faces difficulties and struggles in rehabilitation. During his physical and psychological rehabilitation, and with effort and perseverance, he goes through significant adjustment. He is then discharged from hospital using a wheelchair, moves into a more accessible home, and begins making plans for their future. Bob's life story continues.

Bob was initially actively participating in the Medical Model of care. The acute stage of treatment is over. He has undergone rehabilitation and is planning for a new future. At this time, Bob is not being medically treated, so it doesn't make sense to view his life now through the Medical Model. Using that Disability Lens would be limiting. As would the Tragedy/Deficiency/Charity Disability Model.

This is a moment where an Intentional Shift can occur. The person is at a fork in the road at this time, as they know their life will never be the same due to the medical condition and impairment. But what are the choices?

People often go through a grey period where they are trying to figure out their new lives and who they are. They know their future is going to involve changes in roles, identities, activities, and relationships. There can be a lot of anxiety and anticipation at this time. If the person is aware of all the disability lens options that are available, they can take steps towards the future they want. This can mark the beginning of an Intentional Shift or transformation of beliefs, self-concept, identities, and behaviours. This Intentional Shift can become the basis of the rest of their lives. Keep this idea of Intentional Shift in mind, as we'll return to it in detail later.

To return to the example, Bob starts planning for the future and realizes that being a person who is a double leg amputee, he now has some challenges that he did not have before. When thinking about how to handle these challenges, the Social Model of Disability can be very useful as a model.

The Social Model of Disability

Scope, a disability equality organization in the United Kingdom, has a useful description of the Social Model of Disability,

> The model says that people are disabled by barriers in society, not by their impairment or difference. Barriers can be physical, like buildings not having accessible toilets. Or they can be caused by people's attitudes to difference, like assuming disabled people can't do certain things.
>
> The social model helps us recognise barriers that make life harder for disabled people. Removing these barriers creates equality and offers disabled people more independence, choice and control.

Basically, in the Social Model it is not the person's impairment that is causing the disability, but the environment that is causing the disability.

Let's go back to our example of Bob, who is a double amputee who now uses a wheelchair. Bob would like to go to post-secondary to become an engineer. He doesn't drive and lives in a community that does not have buses that are wheelchair accessible. With the Social Model, Bob's disability is not created by his physical need for a wheelchair. The disability is created by the transit system that does not have buses that are wheelchair accessible. The lack of wheelchair accessibility is creating this transportation disability.

The Social Disability Model that is used here is important as it directs responsibility as to who needs to address the disabled person's accommodation. Does Bob need to take a cab every day to-and-from school, or does the city need to ensure disabled people have a form of accessible transportation? The Social Model would point that responsibility to the city.

Super-Disabled Model of Disability

The last lens that will be covered is the Super-Disabled Model. This is the model where disabled people pull themselves up by their bootstraps and against all odds surpass their limitations and compete in life imitating an able-bodied person. In this model, a disabled person often surpasses what an able-bodied person can do and becomes an inspiration for typical people. These are the inspirational stories based in Ableism that are built on the premise that if an inferior person can do it (ie: a disabled person) then so can a typical person.

People meeting challenges despite obstacles inspire me. Who doesn't need a role model or an example? Personally, one thing that drove me to have a positive attitude throughout my cancer illness was the desire to model resiliency for my son, who was 11 years old at the time. Witnessing other people face obstacles and overcoming difficult circumstances is admirable and inspiring. Viewing people with disabilities as objects of pity and using their success stories to motivate ourselves is Ableism and is highly offensive.

Four Model Recap

These are four very different views of disability, so you can see why the concept of a disability model is so important. No model or theory can explain everything all the time. Sometimes they overlap; sometimes none of these four models can adequately explain a situation. There are many more models of disability than the four listed. It is important to recognize that there are circumstances where a person could utilize several models all in one day.

The four models discussed are the most common types. For people with Adult Onset Disability, I take the view that the Medical Model is helpful when people are in intense treatment for a medical condition as well as when treatment is required for maintenance. Following this stage, people begin living with their new disabilities and have some form of stability. At this point, it is helpful for people to adopt the Social Model of Disability or some form of an empowering model when going about their daily lives.

It is quite striking when you see the contrast of beliefs from people who are not even aware of what disability models are. From my own experiences, the following are actual conversations I had with people regarding my health and disabilities during the course of my illness:

Fred told me he thinks that what happened to me is so sad and tragic. (Tragedy/Deficiency/Charity Model)

Elly wishes my immunotherapy treatment would work better and make me normal again. (Medical Model)

Tim thinks it is really unfair that I can't just work at my job for a few hours when I feel good. He knows that my side effects are unpredictable and episodic, and that I can't keep a steady part-time schedule. Fred told me he thinks my employer should accommodate me better. (Social Model of Disability)

Theresa told me with my sad circumstances and my positive attitude that I'm an inspiration for her to go to the gym more. (Super-Disabled Model)

Back to You
None of this matters that much until you develop an Adult Onset Disability or have a loved one with a disability. Then all of a sudden, the nuances of a disability model definition mean a great deal more. It literally determines how you are treated by your workplace or school, by the medical system, and by society in general. Models of Disability are vital as their views shape beliefs and attitudes towards people with disabilities, as well as influence our own self- concepts.

When adjusting to an Adult Onset Disability, everything is on the table. Our beliefs and attitudes about ourselves and how we view others who are sick, disabled and marginalized. We start thinking about what it means to be vulnerable. As a person with an Adult Onset Disability, it is important to question our pre-existing values/beliefs; as well as to think about the implications of these models.

There are people with disabilities out there right now who have unconsciously and unknowingly adopted the views of one of the four models. They have internalized that model into their beliefs, and now make all their life decisions based on what that model allows. In some cases, the Medical Model or Tragedy/Deficiency/Charity Model have greatly restricted some people's lives. These models are powerful.

By being aware of the concept of disability models, you can make choices about how you see yourself in different contexts. Just by having the awareness of the models, you can start to Intentionally Shift your thoughts, and actions to those that are more empowered and deserving. By the way, if you're wondering, Bob got accessible transit, became an engineer, and lived happily ever after.

Guidepost 3

Be Aware of Disability Models and their Influences

7. ABLEISM AND INTERSECTIONALITY

The term Ableism in the popular vernacular is relatively new. The concept of Ableism has been around as long as people have existed. Despite social progress, my experience has been that most people in North America today are Ableist or hold some form of Ableist view. Most North American people would not consider themselves Ableist. This is especially true of people's attitudes towards people with physical disabilities. I would guess that the majority of people in Canada would not rally against a person with a physical disability moving into their neighbourhood. I would also guess that typical people at work, who gather around their work water cooler to socialize, would say that Human Rights are important and would provide lip service that all people with disabilities have the right to employment equality.

Now consider a scenario where the same people from around that water cooler are now on an interview panel interviewing job applicants; some of which have disabilities. Often, people's attitudes and beliefs become wobbly when they are faced with real-world situations. In this scenario, the water cooler people are interviewing a job candidate who has disclosed that they have cerebral palsy, a speech impediment, and uses arm crutches. People, unconsciously or not, often associate speech impediments with lower cognitive functioning. Efficient communication is typically valued by employers. A person with cerebral palsy who has a speech impediment may take a few extra moments to express a point than a non-disabled person. The speech impediment combined with a non-typical gait while using arm crutches draws a fair bit of attention to the person's disability in a potentially unfavourable light.

Now imagine that same employment panel is now interviewing a person who has disclosed bipolar disorder who is experiencing a mild mania. The applicant is speaking a bit off-topic and having some problems focusing on the questions. A typical interview panel usually considers an applicants' ability to focus on a task. The applicant with bipolar disorder would not appear to meet this requirement. The interview panel, without considering any accommodation, simply crosses the disabled person off the list.

The applicant with a physical disability may start to look more appealing to the interview committee in comparison to the candidate with a mental health condition. However, oftentimes the committee just hires a non-disabled candidate with the justification that it is 'less complicated' somehow or 'less likely to create difficulties down the road'. Assumptions are made that the disabled candidates will require high levels of intervention to assist them in being successful, despite any evidence or discussion as to why these assumptions are made.

In this scenario, the employees who were discussing the importance of employment equity for the disabled were the same people who were on an interview panel. In the end, they all simply defaulted to the conventional Ableist, discriminatory beliefs that are prevalent in North America thinking.

This type of employment discrimination is very common, as is the view that people with physical disabilities are higher on the disability hierarchy than people with mental health issues. Yes, there's a disability hierarchy, more about that later.

Ableism is more than just the discrimination of disabled jobseekers. Viewing and treating people with disabilities from the Tragedy/Deficiency/Charity Disability Model is Ableism. Viewing this group with pity and as a burden to society is Ableism. Ableism is assuming that disabled people are broken and that we would all would be better off if we were medically cured back to typical functioning.

Behaviour driven by Ableism is a form of oppression that keeps disabled people's heads below water. There's the more formal Ableism like job discrimination, housing discrimination, and the inability to access public services. This kind of Ableism has resulted in many developed countries creating civil rights laws to address these more common discriminations and access issues. These laws help to support legal challenges for disabled people in terms of job discrimination, education access, and service/physical access. In Canada, these laws are based in the Charter of Rights and Freedoms, The Canadian Human Rights Act and Employment Equity Act. In the USA, they are based in the Americans with Disabilities Act.

Civil rights legislation is not the cure for Ableism. It only provides a legal framework for which people with disabilities can act against other parties for discrimination. However, civil rights legislation often marks the beginning of a new stage in social change. Through legal precedents, marginalized people can access jobs and services more easily. However, legislation is only the beginning of the much bigger issue of combating Ableism and changing North America's beliefs about people with disabilities. The concepts of Disability Justice take aim at the heart of Ableism, which we'll look at later in a later chapter.

The Ontario Human Rights Commission website has a useful description:

> An "ableist" belief system often underlies negative attitudes, stereotypes, and stigma toward people with psychosocial disabilities. "Ableism" refers to attitudes in society that devalue and limit the potential of persons with disabilities.

> ...analogous to racism, sexism or ageism, [and] sees persons with disabilities as being less worthy of respect and consideration, less able to contribute and participate, or of less inherent value than others. Ableism may be conscious or unconscious, and may be embedded in institutions, systems or the broader culture of a society. It can limit the opportunities of persons with disabilities and reduce their

inclusion in the life of their communities.

Ableism can be expressed in the backdrop of conversations, in passing remarks, or even a pitied look in the direction of a disabled person. These are sometimes referred to as everyday Ableisms. Everyday Ableisms are insidious and can chip away at the self-concept of people with disabilities.

Access Living.org based in Chicago, USA has a thought challenging list of Everyday Ableisms (Eisenmenger, 2022):

1. Choosing an inaccessible venue for a meeting or event, therefore excluding some participants

2. Using someone else's mobility device as a hand or foot rest

3. Framing disability as either tragic or inspiration in news stories, movies, and other popular forms of media

4. Casting a non-disabled actor to play a disabled character in a play, movie, TV show, or commercial

5. Making a movie that doesn't have audio description or closed captioning

6. Using the accessible bathroom stall when you are able to use the non-accessible stall without pain or risk of injury

7. Wearing scented products in a scent-free environment

8. Talking to a person with a disability like they are a child, talking about them instead of directly to them, or speaking for them

9. Asking invasive questions about the medical history or personal life of someone with a disability

10. Assuming people have to have a visible disability to actually be disabled

11. Questioning if someone is 'actually' disabled, or 'how much' they are disabled

12. Asking, "How did you become disabled?"

I believe that the average, typical person is not someone who intentionally wants to be bigoted. The average typical person is just ignorant and unknowingly has Ableist beliefs based on the Medical and Deficiency/Tragedy/Charity Disability Models. Typical people are often inadvertently Ableist and simply don't understand how their words or actions are incredibly offensive to a disabled person. Although prevalent and somewhat understandable to a small degree, ignorance is no excuse for discriminating Ableist behaviours that oppress the disabled. As social attitudes and behaviours towards racial minorities and LGBTQ+ are shifting, so should the attitudes and behaviours towards people with disabilities.

Intersectionality

A discussion of Ableism naturally leads to the topic of Intersectionality. Understanding this theory provides a person with an Adult Onset Disability with a powerful tool in understanding the oppression that affects marginalized people in the world. Intersectionality (Taylor, 2020) is the acknowledgement that every marginalized person has their own unique experience of discrimination and oppression. Everything and anything that can marginalize people must be considered – gender, race, class, sexual orientation, abilities, socio-economic status, level of education, age, etc.

Intersectionality is the recognition of the point where each of our marginalized identities meet. It is an acknowledgement that individual marginalized identities have a compounding effect on each other. These oppressions come from our institutions, cultures, policies, and beliefs from people in society and frame the experiences people have.

Scenario

A senior-aged woman of colour who has had an arm amputation is receiving a consultation from a white, male, middle-aged surgeon for a routine benign ovarian cyst removal. The surgeon is both patronizing and indifferent to the woman and is delaying scheduling the surgical procedure. The woman in this example would be more empowered if she were aware of how intersectionality influence outcomes. In this example, the Ivy League educated white male surgeon's attitude and lack of action is a presentation of his higher level of status/privileges. The result is that this woman is being discriminated and treated poorly based on her compounding intersectional identities.

The woman has several marginalized identities that intersect, namely being a person of colour, a senior, having a visible disability and being a woman. If the woman in the example were to suspect that she is being treated poorly due to her intersecting identities, she can develop strategies to deal with it. Through her strategies, she can get her needs met.

At the very least, having knowledge about why we are treated a certain way allows us to not internalize this oppression into our self-concept. If we are aware of why we may be treated unfairly, it becomes easier to take steps to right these injustices and not internalize them. Having this knowledge allows the woman in the scenario to understand the patronizing attitude from the specialist. It will also enable her to advocate with the hospital for a sooner surgery date and hopefully get a new surgeon.

Back to You

All this talk about Ableism in the world is not intended to depress or weaken you. It is intended to give you the knowledge to refine a healthy self-concept, to be able to face the world (with both good and ignorant people) all with an intentional strategy. A strategy that will enable you to meet your needs and support you to lead a content and dignified life.

It is helpful to know where you land on the intersectionality grid. Thinking about this is part of the process of understanding your post-disability onset circumstances. It is part of the process of starting to Intentionally Shift your thoughts and beliefs towards a better future.

What is an Intentional Shift?

This Intentional Shift phrase has been thrown around quite a bit. Let's define it here. For many people, the life they had before the Adult Onset Disability is very different from their post-disability life. I've written about the diversity of people in the world, and how no one experience can be summed up in one example. Everyone is different. However, many of us have commonalities in our experiences.

Post-disability onset, many of us had major shifts in our lives. Our day-to-day life in work, school, and other activities changed. The way the world viewed us changed. Our core identities changed and many of our beliefs were challenged. The Ableist messages of looking at people with disabilities as deficient, not worthy, and not productive is all around us and can impact our self-concepts and self- esteem.

Some people bounce back. They adapt to their disability and circumstances, take events in stride and carry on with life. They develop new meaningful activities or accommodate past activities and redevelop healthy self- concepts and identities.

Some people with Adult Onset Disabilities absorb the Ableist messages in the world. They internalize harmful deficiency/ inferiority beliefs, consciously or unconsciously. These painful new beliefs limit their self- concepts, focus on their inabilities, reduce their motivation, and restrict their abilities to have meaning and activities in their life.

Then there is another group. We're people who want to feel good about ourselves and want a meaningful life, but know we need to work at redefining who we are, our identities, and our self-concepts. We know we need to take concrete steps to Intentionally Shift/change our thoughts, identities, and behaviours. We need to have the courage to identify what we want in our new lives. We need to make changes to psychologically allow ourselves to take risks and go after what we want. We need to Intentionally Shift/change our beliefs to motivate ourselves to pursue the life and lifestyle we want. A great example of an Intentional shift is deciding to become aware of the option to choose the disability model we look at the world through. This paradigm shift, can be life-changing in of itself.

Guidepost 4

Understand Ableism and your Intersectionality

8. EXTERNAL AND INTERNAL DISABILITY RIGHTS

In North America, I would guess many people take their rights for granted. They take them for granted until one of their rights is violated. Then, all of a sudden, rights become very important. Prior to Adult Onset Disability, you may never have experienced a significant rights violation. This, of course, depends if you belonged to a different minority group and where you land on the intersectionality crossroads. It is well documented that many minorities and marginalized people have experienced rights violations.

I am not going to sugar coat anything to do with rights violations for people with Adult Onset Disabilities. As a disabled person, it's likely you are going to face a violation of your rights at some point in time. It's inevitable in a world that operates with embedded Ableist beliefs. If you have multiple marginalized identities, there are more risks for rights violations.

There are two types of Disability Rights. The first types of rights I have termed External Rights. Most developed countries have laws concerning the External Rights of disabled people called civil rights. In Canada, civil rights have been enshrined in the Charter of Rights and Freedoms, Employment Equity Act, and the Human Rights Act. In the USA, it is in the Americans with Disabilities Act. Civil rights are mostly rights pertaining to how disabled people are treated by society; from the outside-in to the person.

Civil rights are important legislated rights that serve as the basis of legal proceedings to protect minorities and marginalized groups. However, there are some rights that are implied by civil rights, but not directly stated. Such as the right to dignity and respect.

People have rights beyond civil rights. People have rights by virtue of being human that are not always captured in laws. I've split the types as External (outside body rights) and Internal (inside body rights). By knowing our External and Internal Rights, we are better prepared to defend them when needed.

External Rights
- Right to be Treated Equally to other People
- Right to Freedom of Expression
- Right to Make Decisions About your Own Life
- Right to Access
- Right to Safety
- Right to Protection of Information Privacy
- Right to Protection from Discrimination
- Right to Equality and Fairness
- Right to Accommodations
- Right to Choose
- Right to Interpreters and ASL
- Right to Community and Companionship
- Disability Rights as outlined in civil rights legislation
- Right to Add More to this List

The second set of rights are the Internal Disability Rights. These are the rights we have within ourselves and are as equally important as our External Disability Rights. The Internal Disability Rights exist for the protection of our dignity, identities, and to promote healthy self-concepts.

Unfortunately, some people with Adult Onset Disabilities may internalize the false beliefs of the Ableist Tragedy/Deficiency/Charity Model of Disability. On any given day, our society bombards disabled people with the intimations of this model. The sheer number of messages people with disabilities receives about their value can have an unconscious psychological and emotional effect on them. This is one of the reasons why Internal Rights are so essential to understand and believe.

Scenario

Imagine an adult who has experienced a stroke, has left-side paralysis, uses a wheelchair, has difficulty speaking, but still has all her cognitive abilities. We'll call her Sally. Sally decides to go clothes shopping. She has an aid, named Jennifer, to push the wheelchair and assist her in physical tasks. Due to the effects of the stroke, Sally has a few communication difficulties, in that she stutters and repeats herself.

On shopping day, Sally and Jennifer take the segregated handicapped public transportation van that is full of other disabled people. They arrive at the mall. Sally and the Aid enter a clothing store and the salesperson addresses Jennifer, the Aid.

"Can I help you?" asks the salesperson to the Aid.

Jennifer replies that they are looking for some clothing for the 'client'. The 'client' meaning the disabled person who is using the wheelchair. The Aid then tells the salesperson what they are looking for and Sally's sizes. The salesperson returns with some clothing items.

"Would... she like these?" the salesperson asks Jennifer, the Aid. Sally answers and due to the communication impairment, stutters, repeats herself and speaks slowly. The salesperson uncomfortably puts the items down and responds,

"I'll just let you two figure it out". Sally proceeds to pick out some items and purchases them. The 'client' and the Aid leave the store. A woman in her 60s then walks over to them, stops and says to Sally, "Isn't it nice to have someone to take you out during the day? Remember to thank her. In fact, here's a coffee for you two on me!". The woman winks to Jennifer and hands her a $5 bill. Sally and Jennifer then board the segregated handicap public transportation van and head home.

I'll reiterate that the person using the wheelchair has physical disabilities, but has no cognitive disabilities. For Sally, this scenario is an exclusionary self-worth draining experience based in segregation, deficiency, pity, and charity. This is an unfortunate and common experience.

This is a blatant example of the bombardment of messages that some people with disabilities are faced with every day. People with visible disabilities are at risk for facing more direct negative messages than people with invisible disabilities. It is easy to see why disabled people's self-concepts can become based on deficiency and abnormality. As stated before, this is one of the main reasons why Internal Rights are so important. Internal Rights are necessary, so we recognize ourselves and our ongoing value as part of the Diversity of Humanity.

Feminism theory long ago stated 'the person is political', (Napikoski, 2020). I would take it a step further and say *how a disabled person thinks and feels about themselves is political*. A marginalized person's sense of self-worth can be influenced by how they are treated by the people, systems, institutions, and culture to which they belong.

A realistic, and positive self-concept is essential to live as a healthy person. It promotes our worth and shows itself in our behaviours and actions. Having an understanding of our Internal Rights can serve as a key component to our self-concept. Internal Rights enables us to know that we deserve the full spectrum of positive experiences. It also provides us with a set of boundaries when dealing with other people.

Internal Disability Rights

- Right to Self-Respect - Right to Meaningful Activities - Right to Recognize your Limits (emotional, physical, helping) - Right to Assertiveness - Right to Advocacy - Right to Self-Determination - Right to Dignity - Right to Accept my Medical Condition on my own Terms - Right to Independence - Right to Take Risks - Right to Choose my Own Identities - Right for Relationships - Right to Set Boundaries - Right to Feel Prideful About my Disability - Right to Speak Up against Ableism - Right to Self-Respect - Right to Mess up

Majorly and Forgive myself and Try Again - Right to Promote and Protect my Self-worth, Even when Others do not, Especially when I am Doubting my Own - Right to Add More to this List

Internal Rights and External Rights are equally important. They both serve to enhance our self-concepts in positive ways.

Back to you
As part of the process of Intentionally Shifting your thoughts, think about your own rights. How do you express them daily; both internally and to the world? The External and Internal Rights you had before your disabled identity may be quite different to the ones you develop post Adult Onset Disability.

As we know, everyone is different. The list of External and Internal Rights can be changed to better suit your circumstances or values. All the concepts presented in this book are meant to be individually modified to suit your needs. The rights you think about and adopt now can serve as the backbone for your life going forward. The rights you believe you have will determine what choices you make and when you will assert yourself when faced with Ableism.

This process of committing to your external and internal rights is part of the Intentional Shift towards your self-empowerment.

Guidepost 5

Know and Exercise your External and Internal Disability Rights

9. THE ABLEIST DISABILITY HIERARCHY

I mentioned the Disability Hierarchy earlier. Like a company's organizational pyramid chart, there is an Ableist Disability Hierarchy. The hierarchy is based on the Ableist premise that the more disabled a person is (relative to their disabled peers) the lower they would sit on the hierarchy. This false belief continues that the less disabled a person is, the higher they are in the hierarchy, the more 'normal/typical' they are and, therefore, the more deserving of status. This hierarchy is prevalent in society and exists in some disability services. Unfortunately, it also exists within some disability communities.

The simplified version of the hierarchy is people with physical disabilities are at the top (highest status), people with mental health issues are in the middle, and people with cognitive disabilities are at the bottom (lowest status). There is overlap between the levels based on how mild or severe the disability is and if there are multiple disabilities within the categories.

People with episodic conditions or invisible disabilities typically sit higher on the hierarchy relative to their peers. However, one of the biggest factors in determining where individual people 'are placed' on the hierarchy is their ability to communicate clearly. People, in general, incorrectly judge other people's intelligence based on how well they communicate. This is a false belief as a person could have a speech impediment, social anxiety, hearing impairment, or a variety of other medical conditions that result in disabilities in communication that have nothing to do with IQ.

Additionally, the entire premise underneath the belief that communication ability = higher IQ amount = higher value is false and offensive. People who have cognitive disabilities have equal worth and equal rights to have their voices heard, and their needs respected and met.

Back to Me

Immunotherapy is very toxic. There's a paradox in immunotherapy that the higher level of toxicity the patient experiences, the better health outcomes they will have. Immunotherapy made me extraordinarily sick which resulted in multiple hospitalizations and consequently, it worked very well against my cancer. Immunotherapy works by ramping up the immune system to identify and kill cancer cells. The more doses a person gets, the more the system ramps up. This has a cumulative toxicity effect on the body. After my third dose, the immunotherapy overwhelmed my entire immune system, other body systems and my brain. On one occasion, this resulted in my attending the emergency room (ER) due to aphasia. Aphasia is a condition that interferes with the ability to speak and/or understand language. (Mayo Clinic, n.d.). In the ER, I was trying to communicate, but I just could not put the words together into sentences. It was very bizarre. Once ER doctors realized I was unable to communicate, that was it. I was no longer in control.

I fell off the hierarchy. That was a scary feeling in its own right. Obviously, the doctors recognized that I was extremely ill. I was having high fevers as well. I was not processing information that well. As time went on, the fever subsided and my jumbled thoughts started returning to normal. However, I was still unable to communicate. Since I couldn't communicate well verbally, I continued to not be in control of my circumstances. Even as my thoughts returned to normal and my communication was slowly returning, no professional would really 'listen' to me. No words, no control.

The aphasia experience was scary. The loss of my external control was terrifying. Over time, I started recovering and feeling better. My wife, knowing me so well, knew when I was getting better cognitively, despite my extreme communication difficulties. By being aware of the hierarchy, I started communicating my needs to doctors via my wife. She deciphered what I was trying to say, communicated for me, and I started regaining some control of my situation.

Back to you
Why does the Ableist Disability Hierarchy matter to you?

As false and offensive as it is, it is important to be aware it exists. It is good to be aware that people may be 'placing you on its tiers' and that you may be judged by your communication styles and abilities. By being aware of this hierarchy as well as how you may be judged, you are better able to respond assertively to situations. At times this may include calling out a person on their Ableist behaviour. Other times it may be seeking out a different person to communicate your needs to. By being aware of the false hierarchy, we can Intentionally Shift our thoughts and behaviours to ones that are more empowered and that will help us pursue the goals we have.

Guidepost 6

Be Aware of the False Disability Hierarchy

10. HOSPITALIZATION, AND BEING YOUR OWN HEALTH CARE ADVOCATE

One reason I went into such detail about communication in the previous chapter is to highlight how critical it is when you are in the medical system.

The most common form of communication is speaking. However, we can alternatively communicate non-verbally by gestures, facial expressions, our actions, pen/paper, or laptop. Depending on a person's medical condition or disability, they may use ASL/ASL interpreters or communication devices. We can communicate through an advocate, such as a friend, family member, or even via an understanding fellow patient.

Hospitals are like big ships moving in the ocean of health care, providing different health services to all these people on it. When you're admitted to hospital, it's helpful to remember that in most cases they do not know you. They may have your health records, but they don't know you in-person, and they do not know if you have any manners, patience, or social skills. You are patient number one million X.

Unfortunately, when you are really sick and in the hospital, one of the first things to go is usually your ability to communicate. You have to rely on the medical staff to do their job until you start getting better. Once you start receiving care and start feeling a bit better, you can start becoming your own health care advocate.

To become your own healthcare advocate, it's helpful to think about the following:

1. What is your medical condition, and what is the prognosis? Learn about your medical condition from the nurses, doctors, and

specialists.

2. If you are in hospital, what is going on around you? What unit are you in, for how long, and why?

3. If you know you're going to see a specialist, think of questions about your condition or treatment. You can ask the nurses why you're having the consultation and what to expect.

4. Understand your treatment options and the progression of the treatments.

By being aware of what's occurring to you in the hospital and your medical condition, you are better able to make treatment decisions and to advocate for yourself. Hospitals are based on the Medical Model of Disability. No surprise there. Unfortunately, my experience has been that the Tragedy/Deficiency/Charity Model also exists in some staff members within hospitals and clinics.

TIP

One of the most important things I learned from being in hospital and from my professional work is: Don't Get Mad. Or at least don't get mad at the staff. Getting mad at staff almost always makes things worse and usually results in worse outcomes. I was in hospital for weeks at a time for treatment of immunotherapy adverse reactions. In hospital, I found the better I treated the staff, the better treatment I received; it's human nature. Sometimes I felt so unhappy about being sick and in hospital. I couldn't help feeling miserable, but I tried not to take it out on the staff. For one, it wasn't their fault that I was not feeling well in the hospital and two, making them unhappy, changed how they talked to and treated me in a negative way.

Try to be a willing, positive person in your care. Even though you may be very sick, the people working with you have their own problems and human imperfections. You don't want to be labelled as a 'problem patient'. You become typecast and staff begin treating you in a way that perpetuates you to act that way. This becomes a self- fulfilling prophecy that occurred to me on a couple of occasions.

Being your own Healthcare Advocate

When admitted to a hospital, a clinic or dealing with medical personnel, the best rule of thumb is to be polite, but be ready to be assertive. There's a lot going on in clinics/hospitals, and sometimes people's needs are delayed or forgotten. If you're not normally an assertive person, it's an opportunity to work on it or talk to a friend or family about advocating for you. Or try to talk to a staff member who seems especially kind. There were always a few great people in every area of the hospitals I was admitted in.

For people who are overly assertive or quick to anger, pick your battles. In a hospital, you're not at a resort. Some people have real difficulties in seeing the difference between a health care aide and a personal concierge. Keep in mind, they are there to help you, but they are not your servants.

It is a difficult situation to be receiving treatment in a hospital. When facing a new medical condition and receiving treatment with unknown health outcomes, we have all sorts of emotions. I recall overreacting and under- reacting to all sorts of things.

I actually got better at being admitted to the hospital. Sounds funny. I developed helpful 'being a patient' skills. After a while, I started to see which battles were worth fighting pretty clearly. Most of them were not. However, I learned that it was at least worth considering addressing Ableism in the hospital when it occurred.

Guidepost 7

Learn to be your own Health Care Advocate

To refresh your memory, here are the Guideposts presented so far:

Part 1 – Knowledge

1. To Live a Dignified, Content Life as a Person with an Adult Onset Disability
2. Recognize the Value in the Diversity of Humanity
3. Be Aware of Disability Models and their Influences
4. Understand Ableism and your Intersectionality
5. Know and Exercise your External and Internal Disability Rights
6. Be Aware of the False Disability Hierarchy
7. Learn to be your own Health Care Advocate

PART II - MOMENTUM

Each morning we are born again. What we
do today is what matters most.
– Buddha

Success is like a snowball… You gotta get it moving and the
more you roll it in the right direction the greater it gets.
– Steve Ferrante

11. ANCHORS

Dealing with aggressive cancer treatment over the course of a year and spending weeks at a time in hospital created physical and emotional strain. People with chronic pain may relate. When a person has a medical condition that severely disrupts the homeostasis within the body, there can be a feeling of chronic, intense malaise. This overall feeling of unwellness is unpleasant. Your body is telling you in no uncertain terms something is very wrong.

In the first six months of my cancer diagnosis, I had accepted that I may well die. I had made peace with the fact, though I was not happy about it. Surprisingly, I discovered I could accept my death from cancer. I could even accept (with difficulty) the hardship it would bring to my family. However, I found it very difficult to manage ongoing chronic physical and emotional suffering.

Many people I spoke with in hospital who were dealing with progressive illnesses over long periods found the experience draining and upsetting. I was told by these patients that there are many moderate ups and heavy lows during these times.

One thing I found helpful was the concept of hope. Hope that my condition would improve or hope that my acceptance of the discomfort would improve. Acknowledging just how difficult the situation was and how shitty I felt for so long was important, but hope is what got me through it. This is where I discovered the importance of Anchors.

Anchors

It's helpful to have something guiding you in the background while you are going through difficult circumstances in life.

Things that give you purpose and ground you while you face adversity. I call these guides/purpose-givers: Anchors.

Examples of Anchors can be relationships with family members or friends, a commitment to yourself, spiritual beliefs, personal expression of an ideal, or a combination of things.

When my stage 4 cancer was raging through many of my body systems, I developed a strong sense of my own Anchors. I discovered I had quite a few. After hope, my second Anchor was my desire to act in a dignified manner during the difficulty of advanced cancer. If I was going out in a body bag, I was going to go out dignified. And of course, my relationships with my family was and is an important anchoring force.

Before my medical condition, I did not have a strong sense of optimism and hope for the future. I had a sort of indifferent view as to what was going to come. When I became very ill, I had to learn how to be hopeful. When my cancer became very advanced, I had to work on hope as a skill, in addition to accepting the reality that I may die from cancer. I got much better at having hope and at being optimistic.

I'd like to clarify the difference between hoping that treatment for a medical condition will work versus viewing disability as a perpetually inferior state in all contexts. Being in the Medical Model and receiving treatment for a medical condition is normal. The Medical Model works in this context, we just don't want to stay there. We don't want to live in a belief system that views people with disabilities as broken, requiring a cure, and abnormal.

Back to You

Anchors are essential for anyone going through difficult periods and adjusting to changes for a new life. Anchors help us to stay motivated and true to our purposes. I suggest spending some time thinking about your Anchors. Some Anchors may remain the same from your pre-disability life. Others may have come into your awareness after you had become disabled. While still others can develop their importance over time and can be added later. The most important thing is that your Anchors are meaningful to you. By having your Anchors firmly in place, you have solid ground to weather the ups and downs of life. Understanding your Anchors, and using them for support, can be a powerful grounding tool as you work on Intentionally Shifting thoughts, beliefs, and behaviours towards your new life with an Adult Onset Disability.

Guidepost 8

Develop your Anchors

12. TYPICAL PEOPLE, ADULT ONSET DISABILITY AND (INEVITABLY) MORE ABLEISM

We're all social beings. We all need interaction and human connection to varying degrees. The difficulty with being a person with an Adult Onset Disability having social needs versus a typical person having social needs is Ableism.

We, as people with Adult Onset Disabilities, are better equipped to interact and develop our social worlds if we do two things. The first is to understand Ableism, including its degrees, variations, and subtleties. The second is to choose to believe that most typical people are good people who do not intend to be Ableist, but who have unconsciously adopted Ableist views.

By doing this, we can understand how and why people may be treating us a certain way. It will also assist us to be strategic in dealing with others to minimize their discrimination and to help them increase their respectful behaviour. Alternatively, if they cannot be helped with their bigotry, we can decide to exit them from our lives.

Most typical people have variations and degrees of Ableism in their beliefs. Both my professional and personal experience has taught me that the majority of people hold conscious or unconscious beliefs that disabled people are deficient and inferior.

Scenario 1

This brings me to Little Billie. Little Billie was a friend and coworker of mine while I was working as an insurance medical adjudicator for long-term disability benefits. We worked together before my cancer diagnosis. Little Billie was a fun, decent woman, and we got along well at work and socially. When I became ill and was diagnosed, I went on a medical leave from work. Little Billie was really concerned. I was touched. At the time, there was not much hope for my survival as the cancer had invaded many of my body systems. One night, Little Billie came over to bring get-well cards and gifts from work. I decided to tell Little Billie about the stage 4 melanoma metastasizing all over my lungs, throughout my body, as well as my likely demise. I looked frail, pale, and weak at that time. Little Billie was remarkable. She really hit all the marks. Very respectful and empathetic. She expressed compassion and empathy. I really appreciated the kindness and let her know.

As time went on, we stayed in touch. During treatment, I would go through a predictable cycle. I would receive immunotherapy treatment and the side effects would become so severe and potentially life-threatening that I would be admitted to hospital. In hospital, I would be put on steroids which would inhibit my immune system thus suppressing the side effects, and I would start recovering. My recovery involved rest, nutrition and light exercise.

Once my cancer shrunk and became stable, I stopped immunotherapy. I recovered for 6 months and I then returned to work. It had been about 1.5 years since I had first left work due to the cancer. I returned to work looking very healthy, despite still having stable stage 4 cancer.

When I returned, I didn't disclose my medical condition to anyone aside from my supervisor and Little Billie. It was well known that I had been gone for almost two years due to a serious medical condition. People just didn't know which one.

I began working four mornings a week for four hours a day, and I had Fridays off. The idea was I'd have three days to recover from working and then be ready for the next shift on Monday. The fatigue I had was immense from the ongoing immunotherapy side effects, limited stamina, and the process of returning to work.

"Never-ending long weekends hey, must be nice" a smirking

Little Billie said one day.

"I guess" I remarked. After working for four hours, I would drive for half-an-hour home and would collapse in bed. The evening consisted of groggily getting dinner ready and prepping for the next day. The three days off consisted of resting, recovering, light exercise and getting ready for the next week. Ya, it was a real party.

Everyone seemed to be watching. "Are you doing equal work for the time you're here?" one co-worker would ask.

"How much did you do today?" another coworker asked to check in to make sure I wasn't getting a free ride.

"You're only working 4 hours a day for four days? Why even bother" one employee asked me one day.

Having a steadfast work ethic, I always did an equal amount of work to my coworkers for the time I was there. This usually resulted in me being exhausted that evening and making weekend recovery harder.

Six months after my return to work, the cancer started growing again, and I had to start immunotherapy again. The immunotherapy was at a lower dose, but the side effects were so intense and the side effect flare-ups so unpredictable that the oncologist insisted I go off work. This time it would be for a long time, and possibly for good. I would be getting 24 doses of immunotherapy every 6 – 8 weeks until all were completed or until I died, whichever came first.

After six months, I got together again with Little Billie. We went for a long walk at a park nearby. I recall that afternoon I took a three-hour nap before to ensure I was in good shape for Little Billie. I wanted to have a nice get-together. During the vigorous walk I told Little Billie how I was doing better. I told him I was thinking about auditing some educational courses and during my good hours I was practising music, reading, cooking and staying as active as I could.

In cancer treatment, it's important to focus on healthy activities, stay busy, and maintain a good outlook. When our walk concluded, little Billie turned to me and said, "Well, obviously you should be working".

"Whaaaat?"

Shocked and embarrassed, I started disclosing personal information about how the side effects were affecting me. I also explained the importance of positivity in attitude during cancer care. With a skeptical look on her face, Little Billie nodded. I had stage 4 active metastatic cancer in my body, had almost died three times, and was doing everything to recover from my 2nd recurrence of cancer. Now I had to justify to a friend why I wasn't working. I was flabbergasted. I just did not understand how this could be.

Later I realized. Little Billie was resentful and jealous. Some people have what I have termed 'Pity Capital' for others who have medical conditions or disabilities. When these people interact with a disabled person and are in a compassionate mode, they are providing empathy at an energy cost to themselves. They sometimes have unconscious thoughts that they are glad that what is happening to the person is not happening to them. This can create a sense of gratitude for them. If the typical person sees a disabled person doing interesting things, like making art or writing a book, sometimes something inside the typical person snaps. 'I don't get to do that' they think. At that point, jealousy rears its ugly head. The Able Bodied person has a belief that equality and respect for disabled people is important until a disabled person acquires something the typical person values. Once this happens, the typical person's Pity Capital has been violated, and they feel betrayed that they expended empathy or pity on the disabled person. Even anger can pop up when the typical person feels that the disabled person has a higher quality of life than they do.

In Little Billie's case, it was time. She had none. She worked two jobs and spent her free time caring for her sister's two young children. The cancer riddled pity case (me), was doing some interesting things, and Little Billie didn't like it. This is a good example of someone who is usually empathetic and compassionate who works in the disability field, who harshly demonstrated Ableism.

This attitude is especially damaging if the disabled person does not realize what is happening to them. I have encountered this form of Ableism several times with different people.

The basis of this form of Ableism is that the typical person unconsciously believes that the disabled person is deficient in all areas of value. When the disabled person contradicts this belief, the typical person feels betrayed or tricked by the disabled person. Sometimes at this stage, the typical person will begin looking for how the disabled person could be taking advantage of disabled services, funding, or supports.

All of this is rooted in the Ableist Tragedy/Deficiency/Charity Model that sees disabled people as unhappy, sick, unlucky, lacking meaning in their lives, unable to do activities of value, requiring charity, and needing pity. In this view, people with disabilities are viewed in very stereotypical terms.

Unfortunately, this is an experience that many people with Adult Onset Disabilities are going to face. Therefore, it is helpful to be prepared to deal with it when it occurs. It is critical to recognize the deficiency model at work in these situations. As well as the risk this view poses towards their self-worth. This false view can lead to self- stigmatization. Again, the Deficiency Model is a prevalent and often unconscious belief that many people hold. I've seen it expressed from psychologists, medical consultants, senior management, in hospital emergency rooms, in group homes, and in the aisles at Walmart.

This Ableist belief can infiltrate a disabled person's self- worth, resulting in self-hate, self-stigmatization, self-harm, addictions and suicide. It can prevent them from knowing themselves, discovering and developing their true abilities, and stop them from finding meaningful opportunities.

As this topic is important, I have a second example from my experience. This time from the professional side of the desk.

Scenario 2

When working as an long term disability insurance adjudicator, a coworker approached me exacerbated!

"What happened?" I asked.

"This is ridiculous," she said. "This client just got his painting in a prestigious art gallery. The client also goes to Mexico for four months of the year!"

As part of a yearly review, my coworker had reviewed one of her clients' circumstances. The program we worked for allowed disabled clients to reside out of country for a few months of the year. Clients were 'allowed' to engage in hobbies, such as painting. This client was doing absolutely nothing wrong.

"Really?" I said, "Good for him," I continued.

"Not really," my coworker said. "It's so unfair, I'm working full time and this client gets LTD benefits, lives in Mexico for four months of the year, and is becoming a famous painter," she said.

This staff member was furious. 'I'm burnt out, exhausted, I'm always covering for absent employees. This client has a really nice life. Worse of all, she totally has a higher quality of life than I do. And she's receiving LTD benefits!' the employee ranted.

"Ok," I said, knowing something was really wrong with this conversation.

Long-term disability program eligibility is based on clients' medical conditions, degrees of impairment, ability to work, treatment histories and disabilities. Period. It has nothing to do with a person's quality of life, level of prestige, or how satisfied a person is with their life. In this case, the client had a disabling conditions that prevent them from working, but did not prevent them from travelling, living in exotic locations, or painting beautiful pictures.

Usually, there is no 'problem'. Many people with disabilities struggle physically, financially, and emotionally. Most workers are eager to help to the extent they can within their jobs. However, the clients' lives typically don't make the workers jealous and resentful. In these cases, as the workers aren't resentful or jealous, all is well in some twisted, Ableist way.

In this example, the client on benefits was doing some interesting things, completely medically eligible for the program, and had an excellent quality of life. The worker felt angry, betrayed, and resentful. Like Little Billie, this resentment stems from an Ableist view that people with disabilities are deficient and the recipients of pity and charity. They can be celebrated to the degree that they do not surpass the goals of typical people.

Once a disabled person begins to do things that typical people value, things change. The disabled person is now viewed as being on the same playing field as the typical person, but with a supposed 'unfair' advantage (whatever funding or supports that have been provided to the disabled person). At this point, the typical person may criticize the very supports that exist to enable the disabled person to live a good life. It's very bizarre when you realize the contradiction in values at play here.

This form of Ableism and how people with disabilities deal with it can have a profound effect on how people view their own disability, identity, and self-worth.

It is worth reiterating that people with disabilities each have one unit of value, just like typical people do. The value that disabled people have and provide to the world is *not relative* to the lives of non-disabled people. The value people with disabilities have certainly is *not relative* to typical people's moods or their fluctuating level of wokeness at any particular time.

I believe it's fair to say that most people with an Adult Onset Disability would want to be a confident person with good self-esteem. They would want to do interesting things that provide meaning, value, and to live with dignity. The belief that supports this, is that disabled people have value that is independent of other people's opinions. Having the belief that disabled people's value is relative to non-disabled people is ridiculous and offensive. However, this unconscious comparison happens continually in the disability Deficiency/Tragedy/Charity Model that many people hold.

Back to You
This entire concept is worth considering and thinking about on more than one occasion. If you bookmark any page in this book, this is the one.

Having an Adult Onset Disability, you will encounter Ableism eventually. It's just a fact and not something that should be feared. Additionally, it's good to entertain the notion that most people are simply ignorant of what they are doing. It can also be helpful to keep in mind the intention of the person and decide if there is any malice or ill will. I'm not saying we should accept Ableism. We shouldn't. However, in our Ableist world, we need to pick our battles.

Strategies to Deal with Ableism

There are several strategies that I've found to be useful in dealing with Ableism.

1. Understand Ableism and the Disability Models

2. Look for the person's intention. Are they kindly ignorant, like the coffee buying woman in the example in the past chapter, or are they being cruel? Do they need to be ignored or confronted?

3. Determine your boundaries and stick to them

4. Be Assertive in defending your dignity and rights

5. Pick your battles. Some relationships are worth keeping, some are not. If you want to keep the relationship, be assertive and explain why you dislike the behaviour and what you expect

6. Get help from Disability Advocacy Groups, Disability Movement, or Disability Justice organizations

I ended the friendship with little Billy from the 1st scenario. It just wasn't worth the amount of work required to convince an arrogant, ignorant person of her mistakes. In other relationships, I have expended the effort of addressing Ableism and was able to save the relationship. Let's not forget, disabled people are often isolated. We don't want to end relationships that can be saved with a few honest discussions.

When dealing with Ableism, we frequently have to pick our battles. It's helpful to be able to identify when Ableism is happening, as it is not always obvious. Having an Ableism radar and developing a skill set to deal with this type of bigotry is an important part of the process of Intentionally Shifting ourselves towards a more empowered self and future.

Guidepost 9

Be Prepared to Deal with Ableism

13. INTENTIONAL SHIFTING OF IDENTITIES

People have many identities, whether or not they think about them. There are many forms of socially constructed identities such as race, ethnicity, sexual orientation, gender identity, religion/spirituality, nationality and socio-economic status.

Having a disability is an identity. One of many identities that any disabled person has. There is an Ableist belief that a disabled person's disability identity is their primary identity, all the time and in all contexts. It is not. This Ableist belief is especially prevalent towards people with visible disabilities who use assistive devices like wheelchairs or arm crutches. A person's disabled identity may be their dominant identity when seeking accommodations to attend a school program. However, it is likely not their dominant identity when they are on a date or when they are working at their job.

The term 'disabled person' can be viewed as an identity descriptor, in the same way the words 'Jewish person' is a descriptor of a person who has a Jewish religious identity. Society typically does not view a Jewish person's identity as their primary identity all the time. In the same way, a disabled person's disabled identity should not be viewed as their primary identity at all times (unless the disabled person wants that).

How important people's individual identities are for themselves varies greatly. Ultimately, it is up to the person to determine which of their own identities are primary and which identities they value the most. People cannot tell other people which of their identities are most important.

For me, it was critical to accept my disabled identity as a form of self-acceptance and self-empowerment. It has also been essential to accept that my disabled identity is not always my primary identity, and is only one of my many identities.

> I have learned that I cannot push back against an Ableist world and against Ableist people's attitudes if I don't understand and accept my own disabled identity.

I have come to the conclusion that I cannot argue against an Ableist person who believes they are superior to me if, in my mind, I agree with their belief that disabled people are inferior. For example, if I hold the belief that I am inferior due to my limited stamina, how am I to push back against an Ableist person who is discriminating me due to my lack of energy.

In contrast, I can hold the belief that having limitations in stamina does not measure my worth as a human being and that there are many reasons for differences in stamina between people. In that case, when a person with typical stamina challenges my worth as a person, I can easily assert myself to them.

Intentionally Shifting Identities

In disability activism, identities and how they are viewed is a hot topic. It is a crucial topic, as it serves as a foundational concept that many other disability concepts are built on. Some folx describe their Adult Onset Disability as a birth of a new identity. Some folx do not accept any negativity associated with their disability identity. In the end, we each have to develop and accept the identities that we feel comfortable with and that feels true to us.

I am not an expert in coping with identity changes. I mentioned before that I am not an expert in anything. All, I can do is provide you with my own experiences in my disability services employment and my own experiences as a disabled person. How you feel about your disabled identity can be a sensitive topic. If you're struggling with this, I recommend seeking a therapist who has a specialty in Adult Onset Disability. There is no shame in seeking help. In fact, it takes a lot of courage and is well worth doing.

That being said, I have learned some things about Intentionally Shifting Identities. The most important thing I learned is that disabled people are whole without doing anything. With whatever identities a disabled person has, in whatever stage of medical treatment/rehabilitation, with whatever beliefs they have, the disabled person is whole.

The second most critical thing I learned is that any disability identity a person adopts usually has a backdrop of one of the disability models. As a reminder, there are many models, however, the most common are the Medical Model, Tragedy/Deficiency/ Charity model, Super- Disabled model, and the Social Model.

During my struggle with cancer, I tried each of these models on for size. Sometimes for weeks and months at a time. Can you guess how each model feels as a backdrop of an identity? Which one would you feel empowered in? Which model would make you feel worthless and inadequate?

As part of my Intentional Shift, I really started thinking about what my disability identity was going to be fundamentally based in. I realized that how I viewed disability ultimately determined how I viewed my own disability identity. That is when I adopted a more extreme core belief of 'Recognizing the Value in the Diversity of Humanity'. I also began seeing the merit of viewing disability through the Social Model lens. No one model works for everything all the time. It can definitely be argued that reverting to the Medical Model when you break your finger is not a bad thing, as long as you don't stay there! It is worth noting that people often have blends of models in their beliefs, or will have models that I haven't listed.

Back to You
I strongly encourage you to go through the process of considering

possibilities for new healthy and empowering beliefs about yourself as a person with an Adult Onset Disability. It is important to have a positive self-concept, whether or not you adopt the Guidepost of Recognizing the Value in the Diversity of Humanity or adopting the Social Model of Disability. It takes time to weigh the values of new beliefs, and it takes effort to adopt and live a belief. The positive benefits of going through this process are well worth the effort.

I do caution against accepting the status quo Ableist belief that disability is rooted in tragedy or deficiency. This is a very common belief and easy to integrate into our identities and self-concept. It is a very limiting belief system, and it is as false and harmful as the racist and sexist belief systems that drive white supremacy and misogyny.

Employment Identities

Employment for many people in Western culture is a defining identity. Because of its importance in North America and for many people as individuals, we'll go into some depth here.

After receiving medical treatment and reaching a degree of stability for their condition; many people with Adult Onset Disabilities will return to work (if they were in paid- work previously).

Some people will return to their previous job on a full or part-time basis. Some will pursue new careers using existing skill sets. Disability-specific accommodations may be required. Others will return to school for retraining in a career better suited for their disability. Some people will end up in much more rewarding careers than before their disability.

As mentioned before, the concept of 'Recognizing the Value in the Diversity of Humanity' is a core belief that recognizes the value of the diversity of all the different striations of people in the world. All people have one unit of value no matter the race, ability, religion, gender, sexuality or any of the other ways humanity identifies or divides itself.

The 'Recognizing the Value in the Diversity of Humanity' theory recognizes the value of people who engage in paid work. Groupings of working people include: people who work multiple jobs, people who work full or part-time, people who work overtime.

This theory also values and recognizes people who do not engage in paid work. Examples of people who do not engage in paid work include:

1. A Homemaker
2. A person staying at home rearing young children
3. A student studying part-time or full time at an institution or online
4. An immigrant in North America learning English as a Second Language in an educational program
5. A person on social assistance who is unable to work due to a social issue
6. A person working in an unpaid internship to gain experience
7. A homeless person staying at a drop-in centre
8. A person who has taken a personal loan and is travelling for a year
9. A senior aged 65+ who has retired
10. A person who has chosen not to work, who is in receipt of an inheritance from a wealthy family member
11. A person who has taken time off work to grieve the death of a loved one
12. A new parent who is caring for a newborn baby
13. A person who is taking six months off of work for a spiritual pilgrimage
14. Government employees, teachers, or health care professionals who have taken early retirement at age 55
15. A lottery winner who no longer has a financial need or desire to continue to work
16. Unemployed people looking for work
17. A person who has pneumonia and has taken a medical leave off work to recover
18. A person with a disability who is unable to work due to their disability or Ableism

People in these groups fall within the Diversity of Humanity that all have value regardless of their work status, class, income, disability, race, religion, creed, gender, sexual orientation, etc.

The reason this point is being outlined in this manner is that people with disabilities who are unable to work are often stigmatized into a specific 'not working group'. This stigmatized 'not working group of people' are often viewed as poor, uneducated, lazy, abuse drugs, fraudulent, dishonest, unintelligent, have a poor work ethic, and are of low moral standing. Basically, the group is associated with a variety of stereotypical negative human traits that ultimately results in them being viewed as a subclass of humanity.

Unfortunately, it is easy for typical people to view disabled people as being part of this group when the Tragedy/Deficiency/Charity Model is applied. In reality, people with disabilities who are unable to work are simply part of the group of people who do not work for one reason or another. People who do not work just represent one more strata within The Diversity of Humanity. The percentage of people in any individual strata does not equate to each individual's value within a society. Being part of a majority has nothing to do with an individual's human value.

This is important to recognize for yourself if you are unable to work temporarily or permanently due to a disability. When our identities change drastically, we need to reassess things from the ground up to see where we stand. We have to consider how we are going to think about ourselves in the future.

If we adopt the first Guidepost of 'Living a Dignified and Content life as a Person with an Adult Onset Disability', then we need the right mind frame based in beliefs that will help us to feel adequate, equal, and powerful. This mindset is needed to push back on Ableism when it happens.

Intentionally Shifting Non-Employment Identities

An Adult Onset Disability often results in the need for some form of shifting our identities. Accepting the need for a shift is the first step. It is helpful to take stock of previous identities that will continue post-disability. If a person was married, their role as spouse would continue. If they had school age children living with them, then their role as parent would continue. If they were involved with organizations, such as sports clubs or Toastmasters, then those roles would continue. Modifications may need to be made for existing roles or accommodations to activities.

Some household identities or roles may change. Perhaps the person was the head chef in their household, and now they can only help with meal prep. Pre-disability, the person may have taken care of the household finances, but now their spouse has taken on that role. A modification could be that the disabled person now provides input and suggestions for finances.

The ongoing identities the person can continue from pre-disability can serve as their grounding identities. Therefore, a role as a friend or family member could be identified and valued as an existing identity. These grounding or pre-existing identities are important as they provide starting points in developing new ones.

There can be real benefits to developing an Adult Onset Disability. In my case, I was so ill I was required to go off work and was at home full time. As my health improved, the Covid-19 pandemic started and my wife and son were both at home for online work and school. I got to spend more time with them and got to know them in new ways. Additionally, my sister adopted a wonderful 14-year-old girl, and I instantaneously developed a fortuitous identity as an uncle (for the third time). My identities as parent, spouse, uncle, adult son, cousin, and friend became very important through the worst parts of my illness.

Once my condition started stabilizing, I settled into my ongoing symptoms which included limited stamina, ever-present fatigue, short-term memory problems, and nausea. These symptoms that led to disabilities precluded me from working. I started engaging in activities and roles that I could complete while accommodating my disabilities. Engaging in new activities forged some new identities integrated with my disabled identity.

Some of these identities were new or were modified from pre-disability roles. They included: writer, musician, online Toastmasters participant, daily exerciser, family member, new friendship initiator, musical jammer, friend, online course-auditing student, and reader/researcher. Some of these things I only did once a month, but I still counted them as an identity.

Part of my disabled identity was to capitalize on opportunities caused by my disability. Can't work? I'll start being a musician again. Need to be in bed a total of 15 hours some days? I'll start writing a book in bed. Can't go to the gym for 2 hours anymore? I'll walk 15 mins a day. Can't be friends with that Ableist guy anymore? I'll seek friendships with people who value people with disabilities or with other disabled people.

The concept of 'Intentional Shift' includes the purposeful changes we make in our identities. These changes are based on how we accept our medical conditions, how we view ourselves, our disabilities, our new life. My Intentional Shift happened over time, as a process of taking risks and trying new things. I started taking on new identities that ultimately helped to reshape my disabled identity.

I am not talking about big things like going back to school and getting a PhD (though that could be part of your story). What I am talking about are small changes like joining new organizations, learning new skills, taking risks and trying new activities to the extent you are able (ex: like baking or becoming a bookworm).

The changes I made in my activities, roles, identities
were a helpful part of my Intentional Shift into a healthier, more empowered person with an Adult Onset Disability.

And it can be for you too.

You don't have to do it the way I did. In fact, you shouldn't. As an individual, you should carve your own path, forge your own beliefs, and individualize this process, so it works for you. Challenging your beliefs about disability, taking risks, finding new roles and identities is hard work; especially during symptoms/pain or challenges that can be part of a medical condition. However, in the end, intentionally developing new identities for yourself, to the extent you are able, is a powerful strategy for changing and enhancing your life.

Guidepost 10

Re-evaluate your Roles and Identities

14. IRRECONCILABLE BELIEFS AND MAGIC

We all have some opposing beliefs. We all have some cognitive dissonance where we believe one thing, but in certain situations think and act the opposite. Sometimes it is because we haven't fully thought through our 'position' on a topic or really figured out what we believe. We end up speaking and behaving about certain things in inconsistent ways.

One inconsistency I have is when it comes to eating meat. Chicken, pork, fish, and beef are all meats I enjoy eating. Yet, I am opposed to animals being treated in inhumane ways at chicken factories or animal processing plants. I am also a very thrifty shopper who loves saving money. I always buy the best priced meat as long as it looks fresh and is not expired. Deep down, I know that most of the manufacturers of the cheapest fresh meats don't treat their animals humanely. My beliefs are incongruent with each other, and my actions don't make sense.

Sometimes these incongruent beliefs create fantasy worlds that exist nowhere else except in our minds. These beliefs exist solely to protect our self-image. With my meat-eating example, I tell myself, 'I'm sure the manufacturer of the meat I'm buying treats their animals humanely'. I then create a rational reason, 'I live in Canada and there are animal cruelty laws, so I'm sure the meat I buy is fine'.

People who have family members with disabilities sometimes have incongruent beliefs about their loved ones. They end up needing to create a rationale to support why their disabled loved ones have value. I have experienced this 'incongruent beliefs' phenomenon many times in my work with families and services for people with disabilities, as well as in my personal life.

Scenario

Let me introduce Frank. Frank is 12 years old and has a diagnosis of mild cognitive disability. He is a great kid who attends a special education class. He is fun, has a great sense of humour, is polite, and nice to be around. Frank, is the second child of a couple my wife and I are friends with. We get along well with the whole family. Both his parents are very hardworking, kind, and social people. Frank's older brother is in high school. The parents are business people who pride themselves on achievement. They are both intelligent, strategic, business-savvy types. Frank's parents place high value on competition and achievement. Like many people, their sense of worth is partially tied to their status in the world, the amount of money they make, and their work achievements. Frank's older brother is an honours' student, is on the junior Canadian rowing team, and is very popular among his classmates. The parents conversations are usually framed in their belief that people who achieve more are on the top of the status pecking order.

These types of comparative beliefs are very common in North America. The competition inherent in these beliefs is what capitalism is built on. These beliefs consist of competition, comparison of superiority or inferior abilities, and that there are winners and losers.

Frank's parents believe overtly that people who produce and consume more are superior to those who produce and consume less. Period.

Then there is Frank.

Frank has a mild cognitive delay and is in special education. Due to the nature of his disability, he will never be able to get a regular high school diploma. With a lot of vocational training and support, Frank may be able to work independently at a highly repetitive job in a well-structured environment. When Frank's parents talk about him, their unstated beliefs about the world change. When talking about Frank, Frank's parents' beliefs about the world change for that time period. All of a sudden, the world does not exist as a socio-economic class-based hierarchy. When talking about Frank, the parents talk about valuing people as people and the inherent worth that everyone (including people with disabilities) have. During these discussions, their metrics of measuring people's worth change.

Why the big difference in beliefs at different times? It is because Frank's parents have a loved one with a disability, and they haven't found a way to reconcile their own beliefs with having a child with a disability.

Ultimately, the parents' belief system for Frank makes no sense.

The problem is their belief system about Frank does not match their capitalistic and comparative social-economic class beliefs. They love Frank dearly, but they can't reconcile him into their capitalist belief system, so they create a fantasy belief about the world when it comes to him. The problem is, it doesn't stand up. For themselves, for Frank, or for anyone else.

Frank is whole as he is. He deserves to be valued for who he is and as part of the diversity of humanity.

The parents' beliefs about Frank are built on a very shaky foundation. Sometimes the parents' beliefs are challenged when it comes to Frank. At those times, when the shaky foundation of their beliefs collapse, they resign themselves to a third belief that Frank (and other disabled people) are exceptions to society's rules. At these times, the parents believe that the disabled somehow have a magical status which makes them have value because they are disabled.

Did I mention how common these irreconcilable sets of beliefs are? Let's dive into this a bit deeper. What is this magical quality that the relatives of people with disabilities sometimes think their loved ones have?

One view is that people love their disabled family members and want them to be valued and treated with respect despite their disability. Their disabled family members are assigned a magical quality of value because they are lucky enough to be related to a loving family.

Another view of the magical quality incorporates the Tragedy/Deficiency Model and expands on it. This view is that the disabled family member, through no fault of their own, are unable to compete in the world due to their disabilities. As the disabled are damaged, broken people; they are allowed a magical 'special status' and are not measured with the same metrics as typical people. Essentially, disabled people are given a hall pass as they are not whole people and should not be expected to compete in the same races as typical people. They are given a value-lite status; especially made for the disabled.

These little fantasies about people who have disabilities are all, in the end, Ableist. If you live in a belief system of valuing people based on how much they achieve, produce, and consume; you cannot have a competing belief system that people with disabilities have a magical quality that makes them exempt from this system. I believe family members of the disabled who have this view are often frightened that society will 'find out' that their disabled loved ones have no value. This fear is only based within their own faulty beliefs that disabled people don't have value in our capitalistic world.

Despite whatever is going on in the deep psyche of these people. Frank is already whole, and he already has value just the way he is. He has one unit of worth just like every other person, and he has value in being part of the diversity of humanity. This is in addition to the other qualities he has that make him a great, fun, sociable kid!

What are Frank's parents to do?

Once the parents start seeing the merit and logic in believing that there is value in the Diversity in Humanity (or some variation of this) everything fits. The metric of value is that everyone has one unit of value just for being human and for being part of the diversity of humanity.

Ultimately, if his parents can adopt a more inclusive belief system, Frank can come into his place within the family. He can be valued because of his diversity, not despite it. Frank's parents will no longer need to do magic just to accept their child.

Back to you

Assessing our own beliefs about disabilities is helpful to determine if we have any incongruence or faulty logic. Simply by being aware of where certain thoughts come from can help us to start to think about if our current beliefs and actions make sense. This in turn can lead us to Intentionally Shift our thoughts and behaviours towards a life path that is more consistent, based in reality, is self- affirming and supports us in reaching our goals.

15. DISABILITY, ISOLATION, AND COMMUNITY

It is a well established fact that many people with Adult Onset Disabilities experience isolation, (Emerson E, Fortune N, Llewellyn G, Stancliffe R, 2020). When our life situation changes, many of our social relationships change. Many people with Adult Onset Disabilities (resulting from medical conditions like stroke, metastatic cancers, advanced multiple sclerosis, progressive motor neuron diseases, etc), are unable to work. Employment provides many people with a community of shared purposes. People with disabilities who are unable to work simply do not have this shared community that working people have from Monday to Friday 9-5. This can create large social gaps. Communities formed in treatment centres and hospitals are often centred on the person's medical condition. The relationships formed there are frequently socially superficial.

When a person's health condition changes, there is often an outpouring of support from their work, social, and family communities. Many people demonstrate their concern through phone calls, texts, visits, sympathy cards, and emails. In many instances, following the development of an Adult Onset Disability, family and friends become the person's primary community (if they are fortunate enough to have them).

As the medical condition stabilizes, or the person psychologically adjust to their new disability, things settle down and their 'New Normal' life begins. The person finds themselves in an empty apartment or house during the day when their roommates or families are at work or school.

The person with a disability ends up with a very different life than their pre-disability life. Things they had in common with their friends may no longer exist. Past commonalities disappear, such as work, shared hobbies and activities that they can no longer do. This weakens the bonds that once brought some friendships together. They no longer text or see some people as frequently. Inevitably, some relationships disappear altogether and social voids appear.

Scenario

My relative, Emily, was a nurse, married with one child. She was a vibrant, socially active person. Emily developed amyotrophic lateral sclerosis in her 30s. She had a positive attitude, caring family and many friends. Over the next 20 years, her medical condition progressed, and she began using a wheelchair. Eventually, she moved into a long-term care centre. At the age of 55 she passed away from the advancement of the medical condition. I recall at her funeral there was a huge attendance. In a large hall at the long-term care centre, half of the attendees were long-term care residents and half were family, friends, and former coworkers. Her closest friend, Andrea, completed her eulogy.

The only part of the eulogy I remember is the end. It was the part where Andrea thanked the 100 or so people for attending. She told the people in attendance that it would have been nice if they had thought of seeing Emily before she died, as she was often alone at the residence. The friend, in her grief and frustration, began berating the crowd on how ridiculous it was that they attended Emily's funeral, but did not bother to see her when she was alive. Many people who attended the funeral hadn't seen Emily since she stopped working 15 years earlier. Although I visited her sporadically, I too felt guilty that I hadn't made more of an effort.

The eulogy exaggerated Emily's aloneness. She wasn't completely alone. She had an immediate family and some friends who visited her frequently. There was a 24-hour nursing staff where she resided. She also had many friends at the long-term care centre whom she saw throughout the day. However, from the eulogy it was clear, she was more isolated than she should have been.

The reasons for isolation for a person with a disability are often beyond their control (access barriers, financial barriers, communication barriers, Ableism). There are also real dangers in being isolated. Isolation has many negative mental health impacts. It can lead to depression, anxiety, feelings of worthlessness, and anhedonia, (Jones, 2019).

Prolonged negative feelings can result in people self- medicating through alcoholism and drug abuse. Psychological pain can be so painful that people will engage in self-harm behaviours, such as cutting, excessive risk taking and suicide attempts, (Singhal A, Ross J, Seminog O, Hawton K, Goldacre, 2014).

Physical impacts from isolation can result in lack of movement and decrease in body conditioning. This leads to weight gain, further physical condition deterioration and onset of new medical conditions (ex: diabetes, heart disease, risk of stroke). These factors turn into a negative feedback loop of comorbidities, with one psychological or physical factor worsening another.

Isolation is a difficult problem, but there is hope and there are strategies.

Back to Me

In my own story, I stopped working due to the severity of the cancer and developing ongoing symptoms from the treatment. Many acquaintances I had disappeared. Coworkers whom I had socialized with at work, I no longer saw. The occasional text turned into no contact.

Following the onset of my disability, many people saw me through the Tragedy/Deficiency/Charity Model. For some people, I became a 'curiosity' in how human health can fail. Some friends and family members were just very uncomfortable being around people who have disabilities/diseases and just didn't want to be around me anymore.

I was very lucky, though. My spouse and immediate family were a huge support. I had a few great friends who adjusted to me and my new condition. However, there were still holes in my social communities that needed filling.

Interestingly, some new friendships I have developed include other people with disabilities. It makes sense. We are, after all, our own peer group. Developing friendships with people who have differing disabling conditions than my own was helpful. With these folx, I was able to see other disability perspectives. I've always believed in and tried to be an inclusive and accepting person. However, befriending other people with disabilities has been an excellent reveal of Ableisms I didn't even realize I had. By thinking about my own disability experience, I've managed to break down my own unconscious biases on people in many marginalized groups, including: LGBTQ+ and people of colour.

Despite some new budding friendships and my deeper awareness of biases against marginalized groups, I still had some isolation from social and community gaps. I was home full-time after all.

Back to You

Isolation is a difficult problem, but there is hope and there are strategies. Some people who are naturally social, adapt quickly and develop new relationships. Others who are more introverted have a harder time with it. However, human beings are social creatures, and we all need people to varying degrees.

My suggestion for combating isolation is to keep working at building communities and social connections. It sounds simplistic, but that's all there is to it. I can tell you that the worst option when isolated is to give up and to not try to build communities and friendships. Giving up and 'accepting' being alone often creates resentment and bitterness within ourselves. We need to make relationship building a priority and develop resiliency to setbacks. Access barriers, Ableism, and the individual challenges our disabilities create for ourselves all exist. However, people with Adult Onset Disabilities (like all people) have a human need for communities and social connections. This need outweighs the problematic nature of developing communities that we face.

As this topic is so important, I have included strategies to support people in getting started. First and foremost, to make things happen, we need to take risks. Taking risks by showing up to a peer support group, by showing up to volunteer at an animal shelter, or by showing up to meet a friend for lunch. We need to risk being rejected. We could be rejected because of incompatibility with personalities, values, timing, or due to Ableism. BUT we may connect with someone. We may end up being accepted, enjoying a communal activity and end up hanging out with some cool people! It is worth the risk.

I have been blatantly rejected for friendship after disclosing my disability. It is painful and upsetting. And life goes on. I have also blatantly been accepted for friendships with people after disclosing my disability, and that's pretty cool. And life goes on there too.

Strategies for Building Social Connection

1. Seek out people from pre-disability communities, such as past coworkers or people we knew from past sports/hobbies.

2. Family and existing friendships/acquaintances make up an informal, natural support system. We can sometimes develop more community by pursuing connections with these people.

3. Joining Internet initiated groups. Meetup is an example. People join groups based on common interests and often participate in social activities.

4. Asking your support network (family, friends, hospital social workers, community agencies) for assistance where you might be able to get connected.

5. Connect with support groups for people with a similar medical condition or impairment. There are clubs for people with disabilities. Although they are usually segregated, there is value in meeting with people with commonalities and shared experiences.

6. Free in-person classes offered in community locations like public libraries.

7. Volunteering can be a valuable resource for community building.

8. Personal and professional development groups like Toastmasters or the Dale Carnegie clubs are an awesome way to develop self-confidence and meet some positive people.

9.   Disability activism. We all need to combat Ableism, and organizations need all the help they can get. Disability activism is a fantastic way to build community on-line or in person. A later chapter of this book discusses the disability movement and disability justice.

Here's a mantra or catchphrase I like: New hobbies, new clubs, new people, new connections.

We all require social connection. Just like typical people, developing social connections is an ongoing process of developing relationships, maintaining existing ones and having some fall away. We all have a right to companionship, and there's more than enough people out there available for everyone. People with Adult Onset Disabilities may need to make extra efforts to build their communities by developing new social connections. This is especially true for people who are unable to work. We can Intentionally Shift our thoughts, and behaviours to be open to risk, look for social opportunities, and follow through with plans. By recognizing the importance of this human social need, we are much better prepared to build relationships and communities.

Guidepost 11

Create Social Bonds and Participate in your Communities

16. INVISIBLE DISABILITIES

People with Invisible disabilities are people who have medical impairments that cause disabilities that an outside observer cannot notice through casual observation. These are the types of disabilities where outside observers may tell them 'you don't look sick' after they disclose their disability.

A few examples of medical conditions leading to invisible disabilities are fibromyalgia, chronic pain conditions, chronic fatigue, depression, bipolar disorder, schizophrenia, learning disabilities, autism spectrum disorder, and heart conditions. In contrast, examples of medical conditions leading to visible disabilities are a person with paraplegia who uses a wheelchair, people with amputated limbs, and people who have down syndrome or cerebral palsy.

Some invisible disabilities become apparent when you start a conversation with someone. You may realize after speaking with a person for a few minutes that they have delusions, or an intellectual disability, or even a severe depression. Other disabilities are not initially apparent to others, but after observation the disability becomes obvious. Someone with a physical disability such as a heart condition can only walk a short distance before becoming fatigued. If you observe this person walking, you would soon come to realize they have a physical impairment. While still other invisible disabilities are not visible at all, and you may work with a person for years and see them every day and not know that they have any kind of disability.

People with invisible disabilities face a unique set of Ableisms; almost all of which are rooted in ignorance. Some typical people simply do not have any knowledge or understanding of invisible disabilities. These people falsely believe that all disabilities are visible. In my experience, I have found that once the concept of invisible disability is brought to their attention; some typical people realize their mistake and become more accepting.

Some typical people are suspicious about the motives of people with invisible disabilities. Some of these secondary gain suspicions for 'faking disabilities' include not needing to work, collecting disability monetary benefits, receipt of health benefits, use of handicapped parking placards, or for eliciting sympathy and attention.

In disability services, a worker's 'healthy suspicion' of clients is viewed as part of the job. My experience has taught me that this 'healthy suspicion' usually ends up as just another form of Ableism. In North America, the privileges that disability people receive due to their disability are very few compared to the privileges that non-disabled people receive. The idea that someone would fake a disability for the benefits of being disabled is, in most cases, ludicrous. Nonetheless, people with invisible disabilities are sometimes faced with suspicion or outright disbelief.

Typical people sometimes believe that a disabled person is exaggerating their invisible disabilities. There is the belief that the person's symptoms and disabilities are just 'in their head'. These types of discriminations are frequent for people with chronic pain and fatigue conditions, as well as conditions that have symptoms that are episodic or unpredictable.

Back to Me
I've worked with people who fall into both categories of visible and invisible disabilities. I have also been in both categories at different times. When my cancer was very advanced, I had lost a lot of weight and muscle mass, had pale skin colour, and used a cane for balance and weakness. I looked sick, weak, and fragile. My physical condition has greatly fluctuated during my treatment.

However, most of the time I have had some invisible disabilities that were both physical and cognitive (ie: concentration difficulties, mental fog, short-term memory issues). I have my fair share of Ableism stories relating to invisible disabilities from my personal and professional life.

Scenario 1

Before my cancer diagnosis, I went for an eye exam at the local optometrist. The optometrist was a good-natured man, and we discussed my job adjudicating medical files for long-term disability benefits.

The optometrist told me he had a friend who would often brag about receiving disability benefits. The optometrist stated he was really suspicious that his friend was not disabled. The optometrist could not fathom how his friend was functioning so well when they were together, yet was unable to work. The optometrist asked me, how could this be?

I didn't know the person whom the optometrist was talking about, but I was not surprised by the question. As previously mentioned, Ableist suspicion or ignorance of people with invisible disabilities is fairly common. I discussed invisible disabilities and the concept that some people have symptoms that result in good days (or hours) and bad days. I told him that many disabled people (like typical people) like to put their best foot forward, enjoy their social times and don't feel the need to 'show' or disclose their disability to everyone all the time. I also advised the optometrist that some people have episodic conditions like relapsing remitting multiple sclerosis or Mediterranean fever. These people can appear to have no disabilities for weeks at a time, and then during an episode are unable to leave their beds.

The optometrist was very embarrassed. As a medical professional, he knew he should have had more awareness of invisible and episodic disabilities. After all, he works all day dealing with people who have various degrees of visual impairment, and many of the visual impairments are invisible or accommodated with glasses.

This story leads to the prevalent double standard people with invisible disabilities face from many professionals. Specialists, surgeons, nurses, social workers, benefit adjudicators are, of course, people. The people in these occupations are just as susceptible to their biases as anyone else. Most medical and other professionals are trained to recognize biases and discount them when making clinical decisions. I would guess that almost all of them would deny that they are even partially influenced by their biases. However, everyone is impacted by their unconscious biases. Many which are, in fact, influenced by Ableism.

My employment and personal experience with disabilities has led me to the opinion that many professional and lay people primarily believe what they see. This bias against people with invisible disabilities creates an unfair playing field and disadvantages for this population when they are accessing services and health care.

Scenario 2

I have a friend who developed trigeminal neuralgia several years ago. This condition is a painful condition that causes painful sensations similar to an electric shock going through one side of the face. He has been through countless tests, assessments, and treatments by many medical professionals in different disciplines. Despite all the best treatments he has had, he continues to experience symptoms of debilitating facial pain, headaches, insomnia, nausea, difficulties concentrating for extended periods, among others.

You can't see trigeminal neuralgia when you're speaking to him. You can't see into the dysfunction in his facial nerve system. However, you can at times see him grimacing with pain, holding his face, or see his eyes watering. My friend has some symptom free (or symptom reduced) good hours in the day. He looks 100% fine then. One morning when he was having one of his 'good hours' he had an appointment with a neurological specialist. This is a specialist who focuses on people with trigeminal neuralgia and other neurological conditions.

"So not working, and still suffering from all this, are you?" the specialist asked him.

"Yes," my friend responded. The specialist looked skeptically at my friend's rosy cheeks, pleasant expression, and noted his excellent concentration.

"So, what do YOU make of all this?" he asked.

My friend, feeling a bit defensive, told the physician what the other specialists had told him. My friend is a very intelligent man and explained everything as clearly as he could.

"I know what the doctors say, but what do YOU make of it?" he asked him while skeptically noting the perfect articulation, the exceptional vocabulary, and his seamless concentration.

The specialist saw a healthy looking man, showing no visible symptoms, no grimacing, no lack of concentration, no signs of pain. He saw someone who did not appear depressed, who was not crying, who looked well rested and perhaps sensed happiness. Did I mention my friend's appointment occurred during one of the few good hours that he gets in a day?

Ultimately, the specialist believed what he saw. Despite the stacks of clinical documentation on his desk stating the contrary. The specialist 'saw' suspicion. The specialist 'saw' exaggeration of symptoms and perhaps 'saw' ulterior motive. My honest friend, who suffers many hours each day with the symptoms of this condition, was understandably upset.

Back to You

These scenarios are Ableism at play in our medical systems. These are the experiences that people who have invisible disabilities go through. I empathize with my friend. Having cancer, I usually don't have specialists doubting me, as they can see cancerous lesions or scars on my scans. However, when I go out socially, it is always during my 'best hours'. If I don't feel well, I don't go out. So, when I go out, I typically look pretty good and my disabilities are very invisible. It is not uncommon for people to question or perhaps be suspicious of me if I disclose the severity of my medical condition and disability.

It can be a very painful and insulting experience for someone to think that you are exaggerating or faking your medical condition, symptoms, or disability. However, I've learned to accept that Ableism is presently well entrenched in the world. The bigotry against people with invisible disabilities is just one form.

Over time, I have developed strategies to deal with this specific kind of Ableism.

Strategies for Coping with Ableism for Invisible Disabilities

1. Assume most People are Good.

It is helpful to assume that most people simply do not know about invisible disabilities, and not that they are purposefully Ableist. Assume most people are good people, but just uninformed about invisible disabilities. Be ready to educate them is you so choose. Expect people to continue to make mistakes.

2. Decide Disclosure Beforehand.

In advance, decide what medical information and disabilities you are comfortable disclosing and to whom. Your personal medical and disability information is important, personal, and private. It is not knowledge for the public domain unless you truly want it to be. What you choose to tell a good friend is different from what you will tell a city transit worker.

3. Be Assertive.

You may be in a situation where someone is doubting your invisible disability, and you need it to be recognized by a medical professional or by someone providing a service where the disability needs accommodating. In these cases, address the situation assertively with a pre-rehearsed phrase. Ex: 'I have invisible disabilities. You may not see them/they may not be present now, but I assure you they exist, and I need you to recognize them. '

4. Have Limits.

Some people will not recognize your invisible disabilities and will push you to explain yourself or will argue with you. I have found most of these people are not worth the time of discussion. As you've already decided what information you will disclose beforehand, do not be bullied. Roll/walk away. If you cannot roll/walk away, then end participation in the conversation with a remark. Ex: My disabilities are not up for discussion.

5. You always have the three options.

If you are in situation and simply do not know what to do, remember the universal three options in any situation. Do something, do nothing, or leave.

A person is being an Ableist when they choose not to believe a disabled person's claim of invisibility disabilities. This lack of acknowledgement can also be viewed as a form of bullying. It is critical that a line be drawn with that person, or at least within your mind, about how you interact with that person. You may decide to no longer have contact with them. Addressing this form of Ableism for a person with an invisible disability is important for their self-concept and self-esteem.

We, as disabled people, are influenced by the Ableism around us and must go to great lengths to prevent it from entering our psyches and self-concepts. People with invisible disabilities have a distinct set of advantages in the Ableist world compared with people with visible disabilities. The most significant is that we can choose to blend in with the typical people if we wish; like chameleons. We can go into stores without drawing attention to ourselves. When our visible symptoms are not present, we can socialize with strangers and acquaintances without anyone knowing. We can even have relationships with people (like acquaintances or loose friendships) without anyone being aware of our disabilities. We can go in and out of parts of Ableist society without facing the same discriminations as people with visible disabilities.

The advantages of this is that we can avoid Ableism by being viewed as typical in the eyes of typical people. This is a fairly big advantage at times. We can avoid being viewed through the Tragedy/Deficiency/Charity model through which most of the world views the disabled. In all honesty, my experience has been that it's easier to return things at stores, deal with the gas company, or solve interpersonal problems when viewed as a typical.

We want to be sure we are not hiding a disabled identity out of shame or fear. A helpful Intentional Shift end-goal can be to develop pride in our disability identity. This will be discussed in a later chapter.

A Word About Visible Disabilities

There are advantages to having visible disabilities as well. These advantages are that typical people know you have a disability before you start speaking. There's no need to convince anyone of the disability, as it is visible and obvious. This has the benefit that no one thinks you're 'faking it' for some ulterior motive. At times, applying for monetary benefits or services can be less problematic for this group. Interacting and convincing medical personnel about your symptoms can be easier as well.

The drawbacks of having a visible disability is that some typical people, out of ignorance, may think that the disabled person also has an intellectual impairment. This is especially true if the disabled person has a speech disorder. There are many typical people who have disability Tragedy/Deficiency/Charity Model beliefs who may be patronizing or may discriminate a person based on seeing their visible disability.

Guidepost 12

Invisible Disabilities – Have Strategies
to Deal with the Typicals

17. SELF-CARE, STAMINA, AND SPOONS

When working as an insurance medical adjudicator for disability benefits, I saw many files of people who had a variety of physical and mental health disabilities. Many people also had very difficult social conditions that compounded their circumstances. These combined factors led some people to not be able to properly care for themselves. Often, this led to further physical deconditioning. This deconditioning then aggravated the physical condition and created further health conditions and disabilities.

I am not judging or casting blame on these folx. I bring this up to highlight the importance of self-care; especially when a person is under stressful and difficult circumstances. As an example, some people lose their appetite when they are under duress. This is a natural stress response. However, when we don't eat we have minimal energy, we have less mental resources to solve problems, and we become irritable. These outcomes compound the initial difficulties and make it harder for people to cope emotionally, to deal with others, and to solve problems. In this state, problems are exacerbated and the cycle continues.

I realize it's very obvious to say 'take care of yourself'. Eat when hungry, limit alcohol/illicit drugs, exercise daily, take relaxation breaks, get enough sleep, etc. From my own experience, when I am under stress, my tendency is not to take care of myself. I stay up late and feel tired the next day, I don't eat regularly, I do not exercise, and I spend some time in self-pity. However, I've realized the importance of making self-care a habit.

When I'm feeling unwell, I make a conscious decision to 'take care of myself' and go to bed early at the same time every night. Through pushing myself, I walk or exercise for 30 mins several times a week if I can. I try to eat every meal, whether I'm hungry or not. I meditate and self-soothe when I'm upset. Basically, I parent myself to provide self- care. Self-care helps. If no one is around to remind us to take a shower or get out of bed during the day and walk around the house; then we have to tell ourselves.

When I was in hospital for weeks at a time, the wards had big posters everywhere saying get up, get changed, and walk around. When I could physically do this; I always felt better. Mental health is a big part of our health, and employing self-care typically improves mental health.

The point here is, 'Do self-care, even if you feel like shit'. You'll likely feel better. Your body has physical needs to exercise, eat, sleep, and rest. If you can't do all your self-care; do some. Take a shower, eat lunch, brush your teeth. If that's all you can do today, that's ok. People's stamina and independence varies. Tailor your self-care to your own strengths.

Throughout my cancer experience and treatment, I have had severe fatigue. It is a very common symptom of cancer treatment. Many people have heard of cancer fatigue, but few people really 'get it'. You can't just have a good nap and recover from cancer fatigue. Many people with cancer also have limited stamina. As my disabilities are invisible, people don't realize I have limited stamina or that I am tired after sleeping or resting.

Many people with chronic illnesses and other conditions have symptoms of limited stamina. The best way to describe how to understand and manage limited energy is Spoon Theory by Christine Miserandino (Miserandino, 2013).

In spoon theory, Christine,

… explained that the difference in being sick and being healthy is having to make choices or to consciously think about things when the rest of the world doesn't have to.

Christine, who has lupus, is explaining to her longtime friend about what it is like to have a chronic condition with limited energy. They are in a restaurant and Christine gathers all the spoons she can find and gives them to her friend. She tells her friend to pretend that she, the friend, has lupus. The spoons she is holding represent her energy allocation for the day. Christine then goes through the activities of a typical day and starts taking spoons away from her friend. One spoon for showering, one spoon for changing, one spoon for walking to the bus, etc. Pretty soon her friend is down to just a few spoons and still has the many evening activities to get through. The friend is concerned she won't have enough spoons to complete her evening tasks. 'What now?', she asks Christine? Christine then starts taking spoons from the next day's allocation and explains how that will limit what activities can be done that day. Finally, they discuss the toll this all takes and the need for extended recuperation to regain all her spoons to start all over again.

Spoon theory is an apt way to describe how to think about energy expenditure. I often plan ahead, thinking as to how many spoons an activity will take. I also consider how I can balance this with recuperation, either later in the day or the next day.

Spoon theory is also a good way to think about self-care in terms of ensuring we get enough rest and recuperation.

Self-care and managing our spoons are important skills for well-being. We need to maximize our energy as we Intentionally Shift our thoughts, beliefs, and actions to ones that are empowering and self-determining. We also benefit from the self-respect that comes with doing as much self-care as we are able. Self-care and managing our spoons can serve as part of the foundation for the rest of our post-disability onset life.

Guidepost 13

Manage your Daily Spoons Wisely

18. DISCLOSING YOUR MEDICAL CONDITION AND DISABILITY

In disability services, disability disclosure is a hot topic. In employment programs for people with disabilities, this topic is on most clients' and placement officers' minds. We, as disabled people, sometimes struggle with disclosing our medical conditions and disabilities in personal relationships.

Why is disclosing your medical condition and/or disability such a big deal?

Medical conditions and disabilities are personal and intimate parts of ourselves. Sometimes we have our own Ableist baggage about them such as disappointment, shame, embarrassment, and anger. We may fear Ableism, discrimination, or just lack of acceptance by the people we are considering disclosing to. Additionally, we may worry that employers will not hire us, may not accommodate us at our present jobs, or may stigmatize us at work.

To start seeing changes in our lives, it is best to work on our internal selves first. By using an Intentional Shift process, we can develop disability acceptance and eventual pride. Personally, I have had a hate-accept-dislike-like-pride progressive relationship with my medical conditions and disabilities. This type of Intentional Shift to acceptance and pride is far too uncommon with people with Adult Onset Disabilities. I don't have a Super-Disabled Disability Model complex. I used an Intentional Shift process away from internal Ableist beliefs towards more accepting and empowered beliefs. Beliefs lead to new behaviours, which reinforced acceptance and eventually led to pride. As stated before, the Intentional Shifting process has been built into the collective Guideposts of the book.

Through using the Intentional Shift process, I developed a deep pride in my experiences going through cancer, cancer treatments, and experiencing a disability.

That being said, I don't tell most people about my medical condition or disability. One reason is, I value my privacy and my right to privacy. The other reason is external Ableism. You cannot really talk about a disability concept without talking about its Ableism component. In our present world, the two concepts (disability and Ableism) are intrinsically linked in the public's Tragedy/Deficient/Charity Disability belief Model. Due to Ableism, I'm careful who I disclose my disabilities to. When I disclose this information, there is always a purpose to the disclosure. Reasons such as informing a medical professional, to build a social relationship, or to stand up to Ableism.

I've also stated previously that most typical people are not bad people. Most typical people would not kick a disabled person who was rolling by. Most able-bodied people are Ableist through ignorance and never being taught a more progressive and egalitarian way of viewing disability. For most people, reviewing their beliefs about disability is just not that high on their priority list. In fact, it's likely not on their list at all. Long Covid-19 fears, the economy, inflation, extremist politics, the uprising of authoritarian nations, war... models of disabilities are simply not on most people's minds. Many people are still struggling with trying to figure out how to respect the civil rights of racial minorities. These civil rights movements are much bigger in the public eye than the disability movement.

So keep in mind that most people are good, but many have misinformed Ableist beliefs. Let's get back to disclosing medical conditions and disabilities.

There's no right or wrong answer here. In my experience, I have disclosed my health and disabilities to people and organizations and later regretted it. On the flip side, I have also missed opportunities when I have not disclosed information to people and organizations where it would have been in my best interest to disclose. Disclosure is more like an art than a science.

Whether or not a person discloses their disability should be based on what is best for them to enhance their life while having their Internal and External Rights respected. Of course, the person with the disability is the one who chooses whether to disclose their own information. In personal relationships, I use the rule of thumb that if I feel confident that my rights to dignity, real relationships, and respect will be met by a person, then I will disclose to them. If I suspect that these specific rights will not be respected, then I don't disclose to them.

A person with a visible disability (for example: using a walker, white cane, or wheelchair) can anticipate questions such as "Why are you using the walker? What is wrong with you? What is your medical condition?"

These are all common and intrusive questions that can be anticipated from bigoted typicals or by people who simply don't know any better. Be prepared. We do not have to disclose anything we do not want to. A simple and firm, 'I'm not prepared to discuss that with you', is all that is required if you are unsure about disclosing personal information.

In personal relationships, being accepted after disclosing medical conditions and disabilities can sometimes reinforce self-acceptance as you are. The other person may feel touched or honoured that you trust them enough to be vulnerable and disclose the information. Disclosing your disability can bond a relationship. However, we need to be resilient to the ups and downs within relationships and keep in mind that some relationships will end regardless of disability.

Through my own Intentional Shift to becoming a dignified disabled man who is proud to have an Adult Onset Disability, I have weathered relationships that have deteriorated due to Ableism. As I mentioned before, I am not the hero to be used in the Super-Disabled Model. Thanks to following the Guideposts, I just have a good self-concept and pride from my experiences.

Disclosure In Employment Interviews and at Job Sites

Disclosure of disability in employment interviews is totally different from disclosure in a personal relationship. Employment is a legal contractual relationship between employer and employee.

As a rule of thumb, it is best not to disclose your disability on a cover letter or resume. The exception to this is if the employment position was advertised specifically looking for a member from a disabled population as part of a diversity strategy or government-funded program. Another exception is if the employment position advertised states that disabled people are encouraged to apply. In this type of advertised position, if you are prepared to discuss your disability in general terms at the interview, then it is acceptable to state that you identify as a person with a disability.

If your disability is invisible and does not require accommodation for the position, there is no need to disclose your disability at all. Once your probation period has passed, and you are secure in the position, you may then decide to disclose your disability for your personal relationships. I say this not because there is shame or anything wrong with a disability, but to protect you from the risk of discrimination.

At the interview, it is acceptable to disclose your disability if you require accommodation. Always frame disability in a positive or matter-of-fact manner. Highlight what accommodation is required, your willingness to participate in coordinating setting it up, as well as the minimal cost and time required for the accommodation. Disabilities that do not require workplace accommodations and that are not a safety issue for you or others, typically do not need to be disclosed.

Lisa Bendall, in her book After Disability, (2006), provides excellent concrete suggestions for people with disabilities in employment interviews. I have seen these exact suggestions used successfully in my professional experience in vocational programs for people with disabilities.

The author writes,

> "an employer cannot ask questions about your disability unless it pertains to the specific duties of the job. For example, he can't ask (about your medical condition that led you) to be in a wheelchair. He can, however, ask about your ability to type (or do other tasks) if that is what the job involves."

Lisa Bendall also provides these concrete tips within an interview:

- Consider stating the obvious. If it is clear that you have a disability, you may wish to mention it yourself. That way, you can be sure there are no unaddressed concerns in the interviewer's mind.

- Be ready to deal with the third degree. Less enlightened employers may plunge ahead with a cross-examination about your disability. Know in advance how you will handle this by respectfully steering the conversation back to appropriate areas of discussion.

- Concentrate on qualifications. Remember, you're a job candidate first and a person with a disability second. Focus primarily on your skills and attributes.

In the section 'When to Disclose a Disability' Lisa Bendall continues,

> ...some people with hidden disabilities prefer to (not disclose their disabilities and need for accommodation) as they do not want to face discrimination during the recruitment process...this can sabotage a positive working relationship when the employer learns of (the) disability. (They) may feel misled and distrustful. Many jobseekers prefer to be upfront about their disabilities and required accommodations, as it can be a good opportunity to address the employer's concerns. Whether or not you disclose your disability at the interview stage is a personal decision...based on your comfort level....(and) your view of the company's attitude towards disability.

My professional experience from when I worked as an Employment Specialist for vocational programs for people with disabilities is that it is best to be honest with an employer about disabilities that require accommodation. Accommodations vary greatly. For example, a person with cerebral palsy who has a speech impediment may benefit from accommodation of using different forms of communication, like email. Alternatively, they may benefit from the accommodation of disability education, where staff are advised to simply exercise a bit more patience when communicating.

I have found that employers who are not accepting of people with disabilities typically do not accept them at any stage of the employment process ranging from interview, selection, training, and retention. If possible, it is better to find a valuing employer early on. Interviews are excellent opportunities for risk taking and as practice speaking about your abilities in positive terms as part of the Intentional Shift process.

Working post-disability onset can enhance our self-esteem as well as create opportunities for relationships. Part of a diverse workforce are people with disabilities. Disclosure goes beyond our places of work. Disclosure of our disabilities can enhance relationships by creating opportunities for trust and opening ourselves to the accepting people in the world. Taking risks in disclosure can be rewarding in our relationships and work lives. These types of risks can be seen as part of a plan to Intentionally Shift our thoughts and behaviours to move forward to reach our goals and become a more empowered version of ourselves.

Guidepost 14

Disclose your Medical Condition and Disability
when it is in your Best Interest

As a refresher, here are the Guideposts presented so far and in sequence:

Part 1 – Knowledge

1. To Live a Dignified, Content Life as a Person with an Adult Onset Disability
2. Recognize the Value in the Diversity of Humanity
3. Be Aware of Disability Models and their Influences
4. Understand Ableism and your Intersectionality
5. Know and Exercise your External and Internal Disability Rights
6. Be Aware of the False Disability Hierarchy
7. Learn to be your own Health Care Advocate

Part 2 – Momentum

8. Develop your Anchors
9. Be Prepared to Deal with Ableism
10. Re-evaluate your Roles and Identities
11. Create Social Bonds and Participate in your Communities
12. Invisible Disabilities – Have strategies to deal with the Typicals
13. Manage your Daily Spoons Wisely
14. Disclose your Medical Condition and Disability when it is in your Best Interest

PART III - ACTION AND EMPOWERMENT

The most effective way to do it, is to do it.
– Amelia Earhart

An empowering perspective gives birth to an empowered life.
– Hal Elrdo

19. DISABLED POWER

The past successes of the Disability Rights Movement in Canada has led to changes in legislation within the Canadian Charter of Rights and Freedoms, the Canadian Human Rights Act, and the Employment Equity Act. These changes ensured legal protection for people with disabilities from discrimination on the grounds of disability.

And it is a good thing that these changes were made.

...according to the Canadian Human Rights Commission's 2019 Annual Report, 60% of all the complaints they received last year were disability-related. (Canadian Labour Congress, 2021)

The inclusion of disabled people within these legislations provide a legal framework for legal action to be taken when rights are violated. However, civil rights legislation only goes so far. What marginalized groups typically want is social change so that legal action is not required in the first place. Marginalized people do not want to live in communities just because laws say they have to be included. Marginalized people want to be accepted and encouraged to thrive within their communities, cities, and countries.

Disability movements drive change. Disability Justice has taken disability liberation concepts to a new level. Remarkably, Disability Justice puts people of colour who have diverse gender/sexuality identities and disabilities at the forefront. This specific group of people has not been previously acknowledged or supported well in disability movements.

Disability Justice provides a framework that examines disability and Ableism as it relates to other forms of oppression and identity (race, class, gender, sexuality, citizenship, incarceration, size, etc.). It was developed in 2005 by the Disability Justice Collective, a group of "black, brown, queer, and trans" people including Patty Berne, Mia Mingus, Stacey Milbern, Leroy F. Moore Jr., Eli Clare, and Sebastian Margaret. (Sins Invalid, 2020)

The Disability Justice Collective has branched off into different collectives located in different cities. Sins Invalid is a NYC-based Disability Justice Collective performance project that develops and celebrates artists with disabilities, centralizing artists of colour and LGBTQ+ gender-variant artists as communities who have been historically marginalized.

Sins Invalid (2020) writes,

> Disability Justice recognizes the intersecting legacies of white supremacy, colonial capitalism, gendered oppression and ableism in understanding how peoples' bodies and minds are labelled 'deviant', 'unproductive', 'disposable' and/or 'invalid'. .... explore ways to challenge the interlocking systems of ableism, white supremacy and gendered oppression.

The Disability Justice Collective writings share a ground-breaking theory of how to contextualize and understand the experiences of disabled people (specifically queer, brown, black, indigenous, and people of colour). Through their performances, the Collective communicates the essence and values of the Disability Justice movement. With these methods, Disability Justice challenges the ideology behind our culture, society and within disability studies in academia.

As the theories are comprehensive and complex, they will not be covered here. I strongly encourage readers to become familiar with the online writings of Sins Invalid, Disability Justice Collective.

As people with Adult Onset Disabilities, we are members of the disabled community, and we can become agents of change to work on behalf and with the Disability Movement and the Disability Justice movement. Becoming part of these movements, in person or online, can create community connections. It may create new opportunities for relationships and activities in writing or the arts, which in turn can lead to powerful new identities. Embracing these movements and disability culture can help us see different perspectives on our own disabilities and of other marginalized groups. The inclusivity and dignity of these movements fit well with the goals of Intentionally Shifting our beliefs and actions to a more empowered version of ourselves.

Guidepost 15

Exercise your Power: Participate in Disability Movements

20. STRENGTHEN YOUR INTENTIONS

All the Guideposts and concepts are designed, so readers can intentionally make changes and create opportunities towards a more meaningful future. This future is in stark contrast to the Ableist belief that the onset of disability is the end of a good life and the beginning of a tragic scramble for survival. This is an important distinction to make, and it has been reiterated throughout this book.

By thinking about the concepts in this book as they apply to your life; hopefully you've started identifying some ideas that you like. You may be thinking about some tasks, activities, or new identities you'd like to start working towards. The Guideposts are intended to serve as guides, not as commands. We are all unique individuals. Remember to take what works for you, modify them for your values, abilities, circumstances, preferences, etc and leave the rest. There is no one size fits all.

When thinking how the Guideposts apply to your own life, there is a lot to process. Although you may have 100 ideas in your mind at once, the human brain can only work on one thing at one moment. It's not a race. It's about taking individual steps to enhance your dignity, empower yourself, and enhance your life.

One step at a time.

It may be helpful to write down your intentions and goals as it relates to the Guideposts from this book. Another more thorough technique is to write out a working draft of a plan of things you would like to research, to do and to change. Even having a brief plan can be beneficial. This activity helps to focus your attention and to make concrete plans to follow. It can be helpful to think of the plan as an ongoing working draft. A draft that can be updated and changed as time goes on.

The purpose of drafting a plan on paper or in your thoughts is to strengthen your intentions of making specific changes to your life. The changes may be how you think of your disability, your identities, your future activities, or any other area you would like to change. Again, we are all individuals and our Intentional Shifting is dependent on what aspects we would like to change about ourselves. Drafting a plan does not have to be a long process. It can be a brief, but ongoing process. This tool can be well worth the time it takes, as it will support your plan for Intentionally Shifting your beliefs and behaviour towards a more empowered version of yourself.

Following the 'drafting a plan' phase, it can be helpful to start being mindful or consciously aware of what you are doing in your daily life and compare that with what your Guideposts and plans are. You can ask yourself if your present activities and beliefs match your goals. Doing this can identify inconsistencies and highlight areas to work on.

Guidepost 16

Strengthen Your Intentions and Develop a Plan

21. INTENTIONAL SHIFT TO INTENTIONAL TRANSFORMATION

The onset of an Adult Onset Disability is not the end. We develop and change until we no longer exist. People with progressive conditions and terminal conditions are also transforming to different versions of themselves continually.

We are whole through no effort on our own, right from birth, and before and after Adult Onset Disability. We are whole with our medical conditions and disabilities, despite our level of psychological acceptance of ourselves. We are whole despite the impact that Ableism has on our self-concepts and our lives. That being said, sometimes we want to change or improve aspects of ourselves or our lives.

There is a famous quote attributed to Gandhi, 'Be the change you want to see in the world'. I borrow this quote and take it an additional step and say, 'Be the change you want to see in the world, by being the change within yourself.' Being the change within yourself is where the Intentional Shift starts.

At this point in the Guideposts, we've already Strengthened our Intentions, committed to the process, have drafted a plan, and started taking some motion steps in the direction of our goals.

We now need to bring it all together and start working the plan towards empowerment. We need to work towards Intentionally Shifting our thoughts, beliefs, and behaviours. Through this ongoing effort, we will transform to more empowered versions of ourselves.

Michael Sugarman from Disabled-world.com in Positive

Reframing Disability (2021) states:

> 'Positive Reframing Disability' describes the stages that people with disabilities experience. Their journeys are not linear. They progress and regress and may go through stages multiple times and/or simultaneously. Using skills such as positive reframing, opposite action, acceptance, and radical acceptance support people with disabilities move from a negative self-concept to a liberating self-image. By accepting reality without judgment, individuals are able to break a sequence of shame, internalized pain and negative emotions and move forward in a positive way.

In the preceding paragraph, Mr. Sugarman describes the stages that people with disabilities may go through as they work towards positive changes in their lives.

The Guideposts and concepts in this book provide a tangible method for people with disabilities to empower themselves. By working with this material, folx can develop more positive self-concepts and resist internalizing the Ableist Tragedy/Deficiency/Charity Model of disability. This ability to adapt and change is a powerful skill for a population that has historically been treated and viewed (falsely) as powerless, deficient and unable to help themselves.

Shifting into Transformation

Adult Onset Disability has a before and after component. Before 'the event' you did not have a disability, and after you did. However abrupt or long this change was, you are left with a change and all the emotions that come with it. Mr. Sugarman describes these emotions in 'Positive Reframing Disability and Journeys from Shame to Disability Pride Schematic' (2021) as:

– Shame: Individuals experience negative feelings stemming from ableist/societal norms and values.

– Internalized Pain: Individuals define and compare themselves with ableist standards and feel incompetent pursuing employment, relationships, and academics.

– Coming Out: Individuals' journeys are initiated by openly owning their disabilities.

– Letting Go: Individuals allow their entire selves to emerge.

– Pride: An individual celebrates disability rights and independent living movements, disability culture, and encourages recognition by the broader community.

The Guideposts can help us decide where we want to make changes in our lives. They can also support us as we go through Mr. Sugarman's psychological stages.

This Intentional Shift, leading to a transformation, is not anything magical. It is simply working on yourself to view your disability identity in a practical, worth-affirming manner. It is also intended to guide you in living the life you want and deserve. The goal of the final Guidepost of 'Work the Process' is to plan for your future self and begin engaging in the thoughts and behaviours that will lead you there. By Intentionally Shifting your thoughts, beliefs and behaviours, you will be working towards goals such as building social connections, developing meaningful activities or developing new identities.

This Guidepost is the summation of all the activities in the previous Guideposts all in one. 'Work the Process' means to actively engage in your plan and mindfully use the concepts that you modify to your life and needs. The idea here is that you work towards changing your thoughts, beliefs, and behaviour towards the life of your choosing.

Guidepost 17

Work the Process

Back to You
What does this all mean to you?
It means that you now have a guide, a sense of what future you

want, practised some motions in the direction of your goals, and a recorded plan on how to get there. The only thing left is to do the work, or 'Work the Process'.

Using the concepts in the Guideposts will allow you to build a strategy to Intentionally Shift your life in the direction you want.

It is worth noting that if you believe you need to change, but you're not ready yet, there is nothing lacking in you. You are still whole. If you're working on the Intentionally Shifting activities, but don't have confidence in the process, a 'fake it till you make it' approach can work wonders until you gain some successes. Or if you don't want or need to change anything, you're still whole.

However, bringing together the concepts from the Guideposts will support you in shifting your thoughts, beliefs, and behaviours that will lead you to a more empowered and meaningful life. It is worth mentioning again that we are all individuals, and there is no one set of concepts or approaches that will work for everyone. It is important for you to take the Guideposts and individualize the concepts to what will suit you. Essentially, like a cafeteria, take what works for you and leave the rest.

Stephen r. Covey (2010) famously writes that planes are often off course when in-flight:

> The plane takes off at the appointed hour toward that predetermined destination. But in fact, the plane is off course at least 90 percent of the time. Weather conditions, turbulence, and other factors cause it to get off track.

Our paths to transformation often have many delays, false starts, steps forward, and steps back. Our diverse experiences and diverse circumstances influence us in individual ways. Whatever individual goals we have. The concepts in the Guideposts can be used to support the progression of an Intentional Transformation to the life you desire and deserve.

Intentional Shift Process (Simplified)

The following diagrams and definitions summarizes the Intentional Shift Process in an over-simplified manner.

1. This individual develops an Adult Onset Disability and experiences Ableism and negative events. This person internalizes Ableism. For this person, it manifests as poor self-esteem, depression, lack of risk-taking, few relationships, lack of community, and lack of meaningful activities.

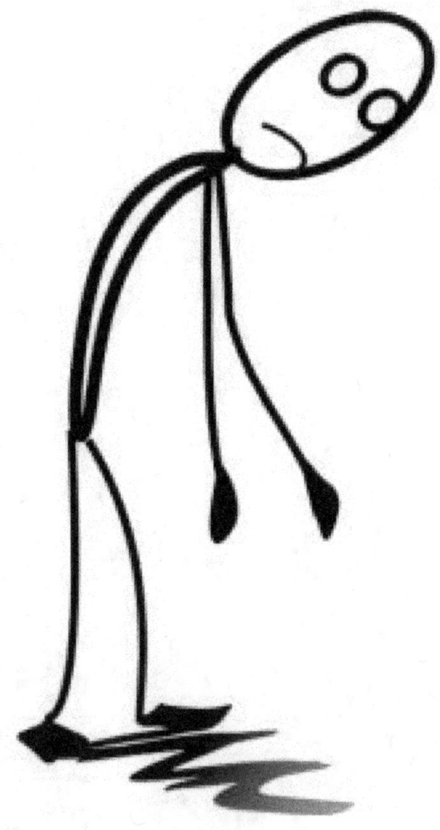

(An illustration of a stick figure with an unhappy facial expression is walking hunched over.)

2. This individual with Adult Onset Disability gets tired of the lies of Ableism. This person starts engaging in a process of Intentionally Shifting their thoughts, beliefs, and behaviours towards a healthier self-concept and towards a more empowered life. (The cane in the drawing is a metaphor for the support provided by the Guideposts.)

(An illustration of a stick figure with neutral facial expression stands leaning on a cane.)

3.   After Working the Process of the Guideposts, this person with Adult Onset Disability emerges with a new positive and empowered disabled self-concept, is connected to communities and people, lives with dignity and self-respect, and is engaged in meaningful activities.

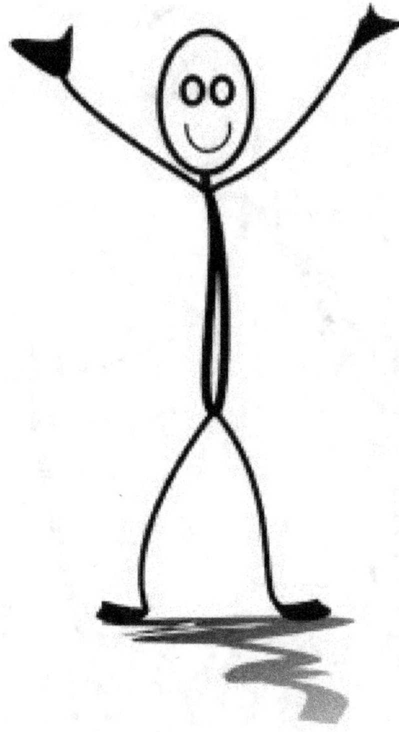

(An illustration of a smiling stick figure, standing tall with arms outstretched triumphantly above their head.)

22. FINAL THOUGHTS

This book outlines many important factors that affect people with Adult Onset Disabilities. These factors are put into easily understandable and actionable forms via the Guideposts. Simply by being aware of things like belief models of disability, Ableism, and risk taking can be helpful in empowering the day-to-day life of people with disabilities.

The Guideposts don't cover all facets of life. However, they serve as a strong basis to help you get moving in the right direction. Positive life changes will happen by thinking about the Guideposts, individualize them, and implementing their strategies in your life. By keeping these concepts in your awareness, with a written plan, and by implementing your plan over time, you will intentionally transform to a more empowered version of yourself. A healthier you, where you engage in stronger relationships and more meaningful activities. Everything at your pace, modified to your needs, by your choosing, and within your ongoing wholeness. The effort we put into ourselves is well worth the benefit we receive in the end. Developing these skills and the concepts in the Guideposts takes time and effort. However, small intentional steps lead to big outcomes.

Ableism is embedded in the world around us. It is imperative to not allow ourselves to be defined by its offensive and false narratives about people with disabilities. Many people are Ableist through ignorance and not being aware of better ways of thinking about people with disabilities. These folx require education and information to help them shift their views. There are some Ableist people who will not ever change, and we are required to take an assertive stance with them. We must also not forget that there are some wonderful people in the world who are not Ableist at all and value people with disabilities.

We know that organizational and systemic Ableism exists. Disability Movements, Advocacy groups, and Disability Justice Collectives may be great resources to access for assistance with these form of Ableism. It is also worth considering joining these groups to help them change Ableist policies of large systems or government policy.

Oftentimes, the most influential resource we have is the view we have of ourselves as individuals with disabilities and of our value in the world. Beliefs of self-worth helps us to be resilient, to carry on despite adversity, and to embrace any fragility we may have. Much like an unpleasant neighbour, Ableism is in our lives. However, it is not ever- present. When it rears its ugly head, we can choose to assertively deal with it, and then return to living and pursuing the life we truly deserve. Continuing in our lives, always in wholeness.

Guidepost Summary

Part I – Knowledge

Guidepost 1: To Live a Dignified, Content Life as a Person with an Adult Onset Disability
Guidepost 2: Recognize the Value in the Diversity of Humanity
Guidepost 3: Be Aware of Disability Models and their Influences
Guidepost 4: Understand Ableism and your Intersectionality
Guidepost 5: Know and Exercise your External and Internal Disability Rights
Guidepost 6: Be Aware of the False Disability Hierarchy
Guidepost 7: Learn to be your own Health Care Advocate

Part II – Momentum

Guidepost 8: Develop your Anchors
Guidepost 9: Be Prepared to Deal with Ableism
Guidepost 10: Re-evaluate your Roles and Identities
Guidepost 11: Create Social Bonds and Participate in your Communities
Guidepost 12: Invisible Disabilities – Have Strategies to Deal with the Typicals
Guidepost 13: Manage your Daily Spoons Wisely
Guidepost 14: Disclose your Medical Condition and Disability when in your Best Interest

Part III – Action and Empowerment

Guidepost 15: Exercise your Power: Participate in Disability Movements
Guidepost 16: Strengthen your Intentions and Develop a Plan
Guidepost 17: Work the Process

REFERENCES

American Association of University Professors. AAUP. (2019, January 24). What is intersectionality and why is it important? Retrieved October 18, 2022, from https://www.aaup.org/article/what-intersectionality-and-why-it-important#.YfwbKGjMKWw

ADL. (2015, June 19). A brief history of the disability rights movement. Retrieved October 18, 2022, from https://www.adl.org/education/resources/backgrounders/ disability-rights-movement

Australian Federation of Disability Organisations. (n.d.). Social Model of disability. Social Model of Disability. Retrieved October 12, 2022, from https://www.afdo.org.au/ social-model-of-disability/

Bendall, L. (2006). After disability: A guide to getting on with life. Employment and Education. Pp. 95-102. Essay, Key Porter Books.

Canadian Labour Congress. (n.d.). Doing things differently: A disability rights at work handbook. Retrieved October 18, 2022, from https://canadianlabour.ca/doing-things- differently-guide/Candelario, C. (2021, March 11).

Charlton, J. I. (2011). Nothing about us without us: Disability oppression and Empowerment. W. Ross MacDonald School Resource Services Library.

Clear, J. (2021). "Chapter 11" In Atomic habits: Tiny changes, remarkable results: An easy proven way to build Good Habits & Break Bad Ones (pp. 142). essay, CELA.

Covey, S. R. (2010). How to develop your personal mission statement. GABAL.

Eisenmenger, A. (2022, October 3). Ableism 101 – what is ableism? what does it look like? Access Living. Retrieved October 12, 2022, from https://www.accessliving.org/ newsroom/blog/ableism-101/

Elrod, H. (2022, October 10). Hal's Quotes. Hal Elrod. Retrieved November 21, 2022, from https://halelrod.com/ quotes/

Emerson E, Fortune N, Llewellyn G, Stancliffe R. Loneliness, social support, social isolation and wellbeing among working age adults with and without disability: Cross-sectional study. Disabily Health J. 2021 Jan;14(1):100965. doi: 10.1016/j.dhjo.2020.100965. Epub 2020 Aug 5. PMID: 32843311; PMCID: PMC7403030.

Ferrante, S. (2022, October 12). 100 momentum quotes to inspire you to keep moving forward. The STRIVE. Retrieved November 17, 2022, from https://thestrive.co/best-quotes- about-momentum/

Floyd, E. (2019, November 13). Accepting reality using DBT skills. Skyland Trail. Retrieved October 13, 2022, from https://www.skylandtrail.org/accepting-reality-using-dbt- skills/

García, Justin D. 2018. "Privilege (Social Inequality)." Salem Press Encyclopedia.

Jemiya Jacob, M. I. C. A. H. S. I. (2019, June 17). Be the change. Genesis. Retrieved October 13, 2022, from https://www.genesisca.org/single-post/2019/06/17/be-the-change

Jones, J. (2019, December 2). Disability, well-being and loneliness. Disability, well-being and loneliness, UK – Office for National Statistics. Retrieved October 12, 2022, from https://www.ons.gov.uk/peoplepopulationandcommunity/healthandsocialcare/disability/bulletins/disabilitywellbeingandlonelinessuk/2019

Ladau, E. (2021). Demystifying disability: What to know, what to say, and how to be an ally. Ten Speed Press.

Mayo Foundation for Medical Education and Research. (2022, June 11). Aphasia. Mayo Clinic. Retrieved October 12, 2022, from https://www.mayoclinic.org/diseases-conditions/aphasia/symptoms-causes/syc-20369518#:~:text=Aphasia%20is%20a%20disorder%20that,stroke%20or%20a%20head%20injury.

Merriam-Webster. (n.d.). Dignity. In Merriam-Webster.com dictionary.

Retrieved October 12, 2022, from https://www.merriam-webster.com/ dictionary/dignity

Mindful (2021, November 23). What is mindfulness? Retrieved October 18, 2022, from https://www.mindful.org/ what-is-mindfulness/ Miserandino, C. (2013, April 26). The Spoon Theory. But You Dont Look Sick? Support for those with invisible illness or chronic illness. Retrieved October 12, 2022, from https://butyoudontlooksick.com/ articles/written-by-christine/the-spoon-theory/

Mobility Internation USA. (2022, October 12). MIUSA promotes disability rights leadership with study abroad advice. Retrieved October 18, 2022, from https://www.miusa.org/

Napikoski, L. (2020, January 3). The personal is political: Where did the feminist slogan come from? ThoughtCo. Retrieved October 12, 2022, from https://www.thoughtco.com/the-personal-is-political-slogan-origin-3528952

Ontario Human Rights Commission. (n.d.). Ableism, negative attitudes, stereotypes and stigma. Ableism, negative attitudes, stereotypes and stigma. Retrieved October 12, 2022, from https://www.ohrc.on.ca/en/ policy-preventing-   discrimination-based-mental-health-disabilities-and- addictions/5-ableism-negative-attitudes-stereotypes-and-stigma

Ontario Human Rights Commission. (2008). Convention on the rights of persons with disabilities. Retrieved October 12, 2022, from https:// www.ohchr.org/en/instruments-mechanisms/instruments/ convention-rights-persons- disabilities#preamble

Ontario Human Rights Commission. (n.d.). Racism and racial discrimination: Systemic discrimination (fact sheet). Racism and racial discrimination: Systemic discrimination (fact sheet). Retrieved October 12, 2022, from https://www.ohrc.on.ca/en/racism-and-racial-discrimination-systemic-discrimination-fact-sheet

Piepzna-Samarasinha, L. L. (2021). Care work dreaming disability justice. Arsenal Pulp Press.

Quotery. (n.d.). There is no wealth like knowledge. Quote. Retrieved November 9 ,2022, from https://www.quotery.com/quotes/

no-wealth-like-knowledge-no

Scope. (n.d.). Social Model of Disability: Disability Charity Scope UK. Retrieved December 5, 2022, from https://www.scope.org.uk/about-us/social-model-of-disability/

Sharon. (2019, November 1). Social oppression. Canadian Race Relations Foundation Fondation canadienne des relations raciales. Retrieved October 12, 2022, from https://www.crrf-fcrr.ca/en/resources/ glossary-a-terms-en-gb-1/item/27044-social-oppression#:~:text=Social%20oppression%20refers%20to %20oppression,another%20group%20(or%20groups)

Singhal A, Ross J, Seminog O, Hawton K, Goldacre MJ. Risk of self-harm and suicide in people with specific psychiatric and physical disorders: comparisons between disorders using English national record linkage. J R Soc Med. 2014 May;107(5):194-204. doi: 10.1177/ 0141076814522033. PMID: 24526464; PMCID: PMC4023515.

Sins Invalid. (2020, June 17). What is Disability Justice? SinsInvalid. Retrieved October 13, 2022, from https://www.sinsinvalid.org/ news-1/2020/6/16/what-is- disability-justice

Sugarman, M. MSW (2021, August 4). Positive reframing disability model. Disabled World. Retrieved October 13, 2022, from https:// www.disabled-world.com/disability/ positive-reframing.php

Sugarman M. MSW (2021, August 8). The journey from shame to disability pride. Disabled World. Retrieved October 13, 2022, from https://www.disabled-world.com/ disability/publications/shame-to-pride.php

Taylor, B. (2020, October 15). Intersectionality 101: What is it and why is it important? Intersectionality-101-what-is-it- and-why-is-it-important. Retrieved October 12, 2022, from https:// www.womankind.org.uk/intersectionality-101what-is-it-and-why-is-it-important/#:~:text=Intersectionality%20is%20the %20acknowledgement%20that,orientation%2C%20physical %20ability%2C%20etc

Thompson, V. (2016, September 8). Disability solidarity: Completing the

"Vision for Black Lives". HuffPost. Retrieved October 13, 2022, from https://www.huffpost.com/entry/disability-solidarity-completing-the-vision-for black_b_57d024f7e4b0eb9a57b6dc1f

United Nations. (n.d.). Factsheet on persons with Disabilities Enable. United Nations. Retrieved October 12, 2022, from https://www.un.org/development/desa/disabilities/resources/ factsheet-on-persons-with-disabilities.html

United Nations. (n.d.). 'we need to embrace human diversity': Un disability rights expert || 1UN news. United Nations. Retrieved October 12, 2022, from https://news.un.org/en/audio/2017/11/635502

University of Minnesota. (n.d.). Terminology. Terminology | Critical Disability Studies Collective. Retrieved December 1, 2022, from https://cdsc.umn.edu/cds/ terms#:~:text=What%20is%20Audism%3F&text=Crip%3A%20A%20term%20used %20historically,regarding%20the%20theories%20noted%20below.

U.S. Department of Health and Human Services. (n.d.). Human rights model of disability. National Institutes of Health. Retrieved October 12, 2022, from https://www.edi.nih.gov/blog/communities/human-rights-model-disability

Wong, A. (2022). *Year of the tiger: An activist's life*. Vintage Books, a division of penguin random house llc.

World Health Organization. (2022.). Disability. World Health Organization. Retrieved October 12, 2022, from https://www.who.int/health-topics/disability#tab=tab_1

Guidepost Summary Reference

Part I – Knowledge

Guidepost 1: To Live a Dignified, Content Life as a Person with an Adult Onset Disability

Guidepost 2: Recognize the Value in the Diversity of Humanity

Guidepost 3: Be Aware of Disability Models and their Influences

Guidepost 4: Understand Ableism and your Intersectionality

Guidepost 5: Know and Exercise your External and Internal Disability Rights

Guidepost 6: Be Aware of the False Disability Hierarchy

Guidepost 7: Learn to be your own Health Care Advocate

Part II – Momentum

Guidepost 8: Develop your Anchors

Guidepost 9: Be Prepared to Deal with Ableism

Guidepost 10: Re-evaluate your Roles and Identities

Guidepost 11: Create Social Bonds and Participate in your Communities

Guidepost 12: Invisible Disabilities – Have Strategies to Deal with the Typicals

Part III – Action and Empowerment

ACKNOWLEDGEMENT

This book would not be possible without the unending support, love, and talent of my beautiful wife and co-author, L Kuhn. She provided endless feedback, edits, formatting, and writing brilliance. I, MJ, the 'sloppy architect' of this book, developed the Guideposts from the journals I wrote throughout my stage 4 cancer and disability journey. My wife helped finesse them into readable form.

This book was inspired by the following authors and their writings. The fearless book 'Care Work: Dreaming Disability Justice (2018),' by Leah Lakshmi Piepzna-Samarasinha sparked my own passion and inspiration. 'Nothing About Us Without Us: Disability Oppression and Empowerment (1998),' by James I. Charleton provided an intellectual perspective that enhanced my own view. Alice Wong's Year of the Tiger: An Activist's Life (2022) demonstrated a powerful and helpful narrative.

The writings of Micheal Sugarman on disabledworld.com, that were discovered late in the book writing process, provided a unique validation that many of Disabled 101's concepts are universal in the experiences of people with disabilities. Mr. Sugarman's concepts offered differing contexts and views that helped reshape my own.

A special thank you to my son, niece, sister, parents, cousin, and wife's parents who were so helpful during the most difficult periods of my cancer journey.

www.ingramcontent.com/pod-product-compliance
Lightning Source LLC
Chambersburg PA
CBHW071024250726
48653CB00005B/1697